Love and Sex in a New Relationship

Love and Sex in a New Relationship explores leaving a long relationship and starting a new one, with all the complexities that entails. Using her experience as a relationship therapist, Cate Campbell takes the reader through the journey of loss and renewal, examining the dynamics involved in the end and beginning of a relationship, and how to give new relationships the best chance of survival.

Focusing on three main relationship issues, the book considers: how to end a relationship and manage ongoing contact with an ex; how to understand what went wrong in previous relationships; and how to overcome everyday relationship problems and make relationships thrive. Taking into account the effect of technology and social media, and how to make online dating work, the book offers a distinctly modern take on relationships. Similarly, the spectrum of sexuality, gender and sexual relationships is addressed, with many different examples included throughout the book.

With practical advice, case studies, quizzes and exercises to help identify and remedy a variety of problems that can occur at any stage of a relationship, *Love and Sex in a New Relationship* will provide an essential resource for relationship counsellors and their clients.

Cate Campbell is a relationship and psychosexual therapist, lecturer with the Foundation for Counselling & Relationship Studies and a clinical manager with Relate.

D1452436

Love and Sex in a
New Relationship

Cate Campbell

Routledge
Taylor & Francis Group

LONDON AND NEW YORK

First published 2018
by Routledge
2 Park Square, Milton Park, Abingdon, Oxon OX14 4RN

and by Routledge
711 Third Avenue, New York, NY 10017

Routledge is an imprint of the Taylor & Francis Group, an informa business

© 2018 Cate Campbell

British Library Cataloguing in Publication Data
A catalogue record for this book is available from the British Library

Library of Congress Cataloging in Publication Data
Names: Campbell, Cate (Relationship therapist), author.
Title: Love and sex in a new relationship / Cate Campbell.
Description: 1 Edition. | New York : Routledge, [2018] | Includes index.
Identifiers: LCCN 2017039777 | ISBN 9780415788717 (hardback) |
ISBN 9780415788724 (pbk.) | ISBN 9781351213622 (Master) |
ISBN 9781351213615 (Web) | ISBN 9781351213608 (epub) |
ISBN 9781351213592 (mobipocket)
Subjects: LCSH: Interpersonal relations. | Love. | Intimacy (Psychology)
Classification: LCC HM1106 .C367 2018 | DDC 302–dc23
LC record available at https://lccn.loc.gov/2017039777

ISBN: 978-0-415-78871-7 (hbk)
ISBN: 978-0-415-78872-4 (pbk)
ISBN: 978-1-351-21362-2 (ebk)

Typeset in Sabon
by Out of House Publishing

Contents

PART III
Managing new relationships 115

Exercises

Quizzes

Introduction

Once upon a time you probably had a clear vision of the way a for-ever relationship should be. If you've since experienced a relation-ship breakup, you may now be much less certain, if not completely disenchanted. You may have consoled yourself that you just chose the wrong relationship and so still have faith that wanting some-thing badly enough can make it happen. Or you may be completely disillusioned and feel that risking another relationship is just asking for trouble. Whether you find yourself hopeful and idealistic, disap-pointed and embittered or somewhere in-between, it's likely your thoughts and feelings have been affected by the way we're encour-aged to think about love and relationships – particularly the idea that love conquers all.

Fairy tales have a great deal to answer for. If only it were true that we would all one day meet a handsome prince or princess – some-times cunningly disguised as a frog, ogre or beast – and ride off into the sunset to live happily ever after with no money troubles, snor-ing, arguing, infertility, illness or sexual problems to muck things up. Sadly, real life rarely goes this smoothly. In the UK, 40 per cent of marriages end before the couple reach their twentieth wedding anniversary, due to death (6 per cent) and divorce (34 per cent), according to the Office for National Statistics. Overall, in England and Wales 42 per cent of marriages currently end in divorce, and about a third of over-fifties are single.

The danger years for divorce are in the first decade of marriage, with a 3 per cent risk between years four and eight. However, the percentage *increase* in divorce is highest in older couples and continuing to rise, with a projection that by 2037 almost one in ten couples divorcing will be aged more than 60. These fig-ures don't take into account couples who have separated but not formally divorced. It's also impossible to know how many of the 10 per cent of cohabiting couples end up separating, though they may be similar numbers to those who divorce. That's an awful lot of people with shattered dreams, struggling to rebuild their lives in a world they may feel has changed considerably since the last time they were dating. Whatever your age, the world can look and feel very different when you emerge from a broken relationship.

As well as the many practical complexities you must negotiate, you may find yourself repositioned in the eyes of others – whether liberated from a toxic relationship or grieving for a lost love, many people find it harder than expected to settle into a new role. Though you are joining a growing army of exes, you may find it difficult to share your vulnerabilities or to know when and where it's appropriate to do so. In an attempt to avoid others' pity, you may develop a sort of emotional armour that makes you seem full of confidence and that belies your real doubts. Some people feel frozen and unable to move on, different from those around them and overflowing with bitterness. Others leap into love again without a thought for the consequences.

There are infinite ways to respond to the end of a relationship and no template to help you reposition yourself. However, most people need time to make the shift from together to apart, and it can be difficult to get rid of unhelpful thoughts about what you've been through and what may still be to come. Being fearful is natural, so it's probably wiser to be cautious, take your time and make no rash decisions in the heat of a difficult moment.

For those whose partner has died, the sense of loss may make it impossible to imagine the future at all, let alone another relationship. If your future had been planned, and especially if the death was unexpected, you may feel cheated and bereft yet long for companionship and love.

For some people, a new relationship as soon as possible may seem like the answer or you may feel you're done with love forever. However you feel about the idea, you'll almost certainly worry about repeating mistakes, and blame yourself or your ex-partner without seeing the role you both had to play. Many people also find it hard to accept that some initially great relationships just run out of steam. Couples who continue to get along well, but have lost their spark, are often criticised by others who can't understand why they're splitting if they're still friends.

Even though Happy Ever After is the real fairy tale, we're still inclined to believe in it, worrying that anything less than perfect is either not worth having or reflects our worth, and that love can fix anything if we just try hard enough. Couples are bombarded with messages telling them what their relationship should be like, and probably just as many telling them how to fix whatever is less than ideal. What's more, many second-timers are unprepared for their new relationship to be played out publicly on social media, unwittingly inviting judgement and requiring a new set of rules and protocol. Many couples either once again cross their fingers and hope for the best – even though this time round they're carrying more baggage and less energy – or just lose their nerve and back out.

Part of the problem may be not knowing what to expect or where to turn. Friends, family and the media may be full of advice on relaunching as a single, and even trying to set you up with someone new, but they don't always take into account mixed feelings and fears. What you probably want to know is how to manage your approach to embarking on another relationship, and particularly how to learn from the experience of the past. This book is aimed to give you the information you need to make preferred choices from an informed position, particularly the second time.

From my experience as a relationship therapist, I know that most people are desperate to understand the reasons behind their own and their partner's behaviour and to have some answers to why relationships flounder. Many look for a way to create a code of conduct for themselves that keeps them safe, knowledgeable about themselves and their partners, with the means to understand and tackle difficulties. This book sets out to do just that.

The book is in three parts, with the first section, 'A new start', exploring the experiences of loss and renewal associated with the end of a relationship, while looking realistically at what's needed going forward. Whatever the reason for the ending, this section looks at ways to manage the relationship with your ex and how to find the most comfortable and helpful way to proceed with your own life. Chapter 1, on making decisions, considers the process of breaking up and some sources of support, while Chapter 2 discusses how to manage the relationship with your ex as you separate and beyond. The final chapter in the section, about your single self, considers self-care, giving some practical advice about resuming dating, including online dating, managing social media, safe sex and body consciousness.

As you move forward from a long relationship, you may be keen to understand more about why it ended and to learn from this. Consequently, the second section, 'Looking forward – looking back', explores the way relationships are conducted. Chapter 4 explains how the past can influence beliefs, expectations and the way we behave in relationships, offering some ideas to help become more aware of motivation and behaviour. Building on this, in Chapter 5, we learn why couples argue, with some suggestions of ways to change negative relationship dynamics. Much of what we do in relationships happens outside our awareness, so Chapter 6 considers the unconscious contract between couples that keeps them repeating the same behaviours, whether or not these are helpful. Chapter 7 completes this section by examining the way unfinished business from the past can affect current relationships.

'Managing new relationships' is the focus of Part III, beginning in Chapter 8 with what may seem a surprising explanation of the way uncertainty can be good for relationships and a detailed look at how each partner can learn to manage insecurity and stress. The section continues in Chapter 9, offering advice on breaking and avoiding harmful relationship patterns and improving communication. Chapter 10, on relationship trauma, explores other ways couples sometimes hurt each other, often unintentionally, and how this can be dealt with. How previous hurts can be triggered in new relationships and changing circumstances are also addressed, such as when a partner's sexuality alters or whose porn use becomes compulsive. Sex is the focus of Chapter 11, considering the issues that may be of concern as you relaunch into the world of dating. Chapter 12 considers the relationship lifecycle, looking at what you can expect, the variety of challenges you may experience and offering some ideas for negotiating your way through. The final chapter tackles the everyday challenge of life with a partner, offering strategies to keep the relationship going so that you're able to create your own Happy Ever After.

As well as offering down-to-earth information about what makes a solid relationship and why relationships encounter difficulties, the book offers help to explore your own experience, as well as offering advice and solutions. This could also improve other relationships and areas of life, such as work and self-esteem. The chapters build on each other, and cross-referencing to other sections will allow you to find what you need easily, so you can dip in and out as well as read from cover to cover. Throughout the book there are exercises and quizzes to help guide you, as well as case studies based on real-life couples' experiences.

The book is grounded in feedback and results from experience with couples, using what has helped them most to improve their lives and relationships, as well as tried-and-tested theory and research. In my work with couples, I have often wished they could all have the experience and knowledge that relationship counsellors acquire. This book is an attempt to share that, so it will be a resource for therapists working with couples too. For most readers, it will offer a different way of thinking about couple issues that, I hope, will help you work confidently towards the kind of relationship that suits you best.

Part I

A new start

Chapter 1

Making decisions

Living happily ever after is a lovely idea – once you find true love you can live safe and sound in a castle where there'll be no more fire-breathing dragons or wicked witches around, and you'll just be able to relax and never have to worry again... Except that commitment to another person doesn't necessarily pull up the drawbridge on all the less-pleasant aspects of life. There may not be fire-breathing dragons in your world, but we don't leave anxiety, depression or unhelpful thinking at the altar. And while there may be no cackling harridans with broomsticks, it's easy to blame other people or bad luck for putting a spell on our happiness. In fact, when things aren't quite as perfect as we'd hoped, the easiest person to blame is often our partner.

With so much going on in our lives, working out whether a relationship is worth persisting with can be very difficult or just require too much energy. Even when they're miserable, most people don't just drop their relationship if the going gets a little tough, particularly when they've set up home together. In fact, many of us keep plugging on long beyond the point when the relationship is salvageable, enduring years of misery and diminishing each other's self-esteem and wellbeing. If you're considering ending a relationship, it can be helpful to work out what's been keeping it going so far.

Why rock the boat?

You're not wildly happy, but you have a comfortable home and a pleasant lifestyle. True, you pretty much live separate lives and rarely make love, but there's nothing awful happening. You just sometimes wonder what else is out there.

Many people rub along comfortably like this. Often, a positive relationship loses the spark it once had. This could be because you've given up hope that change is possible or, more likely, that you've both grown and changed in a nurturing relationship and now don't actually need it in the same way.

If you're good friends and feel your emotional needs are fulfilled, you'll probably want to stay put. But one or both of you may have a hankering for a new relationship that offers potential for the next stage of your life. Before settling for less than you want or cutting loose, it's worth exploring the kind of relationship you'd both be comfortable with if you stayed together. It may be that developing other friendships or interests would satisfy the longing part of you that still needs more. Perhaps changes within the relationship would meet more of your needs. Or you may decide you do want to separate, but can stay the best of friends.

Better the devil you know

You feel you've had similar relationships in the past, that you make bad relationship choices or that you make the same mistakes in relationships, so starting again really wouldn't change anything.

We're often drawn to people who hold out hope for change, but who actually keep us locked into unhelpful patterns of behaviour that may have begun in childhood. However, what was appropriate in childhood often doesn't work in an adult relationship. We just don't know how to be different – that's why we look for a nurturing relationship which will help us to change. Often, though, we bond with someone who has similar or connecting issues. We're then angry with each other when we don't move on, and we stay locked in a never-ending sequence of disappointment and anger. For instance, it's common for couples not to tell each other what they want or need but to then be disappointed when their needs aren't met. However, if one of you changes, the other will most likely respond differently too. Being clearer about your needs, and appreciative when they're met, is likely to result in more co-operation and less arguing. This may ultimately result in the devil you know becoming the devil you *want* to know.

Separation equals failure

You expected this relationship to be forever; separation would make people think you weren't 'good enough' to keep a partner or that you haven't tried hard enough.

People often feel like this when they have fundamental negative beliefs about themselves and expect to be judged. Actually, though, if your relationship has run its course, and you've grown and developed to the point where you need something different, surely the relationship *has* been successful; the years behind you are testimony to this.

You can't face going through a breakup

Especially if you've been through an unpleasant split in the past, you may fear the process of parting.

There's no need for so many relationship splits to be as ugly as they often are, but fear of the separation process makes many people stay in unhappy relationships long beyond their natural ending. Antagonism and resentment may be intense and lead to tit-for-tat recriminations and nastiness. Sometimes, though, separating couples find anger easier to manage than the grief and nostalgia that might surface if they stopped being angry. Realising that the sadness of parting has to be faced, even if you can't wait to get away, can actually make the process more bearable.

You're afraid of being alone

You're worried about loneliness, coping financially, managing your household and the effect on other relationships.

Worry about being unable to cope alone is very natural, especially if you've been in a long relationship. However, separated people do cope and are often surprised at how much happier they are. Don't make up your mind that you won't manage without first investigating what life might be like – how much money you could have, where you could live and so on. Very commonly, people only believe they wouldn't survive because their partners have told them so.

You have nowhere else to go

It's difficult when you have to continue cohabiting while you wait to sell your home or find somewhere else to live, but indefinitely living together when you're both unhappy is even harder. It probably isn't a good idea to try to carry on living together in just the same way as before, especially if you're timing a legal separation. You'll need to agree how this is to work, whether you each occupy different areas of the house, when you have friends to visit, kitchen and childcare arrangements and so on.

You may not be financially worse off. If you have children and are living together but are officially separated, you may be able to claim benefits. If your partner moves out, don't forget to tell relevant agencies, such as insurers, tax and social security, and remember to claim your council tax discount. The domestic violence charity Refuge has a downloadable leaflet, *You Can Afford To Leave* (www.refuge.org.uk).

Family and friends would be shocked

Your family and friends all love your partner and see you as the perfect couple.

Even very close family and friends don't know what your relationship is really like, particularly if you've been trying to give a positive impression. This is especially common when partners feel ashamed that their relationship isn't as happy as it 'should' be. In abusive relationships, both partners may feel shame and collude to cover up what's going on so well that family and friends have no idea of the misery involved. Try telling them what's really happening, making clear that this isn't new.

Any relationship is better than none

Again, you dread being judged for being alone and fear you won't cope. Perhaps your family and friends have cultural or religious reasons for wanting you to be married.

Other people don't know what your relationship's like – only you do. Damaging relationships don't just harm one or both partners, they also affect children and, ultimately, *their* relationships in years to come. Telling a variety of people what you're experiencing will give you a more balanced and broader view. It's likely that you'll find people who think you've tried hard and deserve better.

No one else would put up with you

You don't feel lovable and fear no one else will ever want you.

Feeling unlovable stems from a fundamental lack of self-esteem, and leaves you open to abuse. If you feel you're being taken advantage of or belittled, if your partner ridicules or ignores you rather than trying to reassure you when you're sad or in need, if however hard you try you still don't come up to scratch, then it's your partner – not you – that no one else would put up with.

Stay for the children's sake

Your children adore your partner and you don't want to deprive them of this relationship, nor do you want to see less of them yourself.

Actually, there's considerable evidence that children in conflicted families often wish their parents would split. Institute of Fiscal Studies research suggests that the effects on children depend on the characteristics of the parents, and that separation doesn't in itself have negative effects on their development. What children want and need most is stability and consistency and for their parents to get on, which is sometimes only possible once they separate. Even if you see the children less often, the time you have together may be more pleasant and focused. You may appreciate the break from them too, giving you the chance to do things for yourself.

Your partner would be devastated

Your partner seems very fragile and has intimated that they couldn't go on if the relationship were to end.

No doubt your partner *will* be upset if you split, but continuing in a relationship that isn't working is upsetting too. Threatening anything – including self-harm – is abusive and completely unconducive to the continuance of a mature, healthy relationship. Your relationship could even be better following the breakup. Many ex-partners remain lifelong friends, and this may be something you could emphasise and work towards. Counselling support, both as a couple and individually, also helps couples manage separation. This is the time to make the most of any family and friends who are willing to rally round too. Separating is tough, but usually better than struggling to maintain a relationship that's on its knees.

It's not like it was at the beginning

The early days of your relationship were full of excitement, you had your head in the clouds and felt more in love than you could imagine. Now that feeling has gone, you wonder if this is love after all.

When you meet a new partner with the potential to meet your emotional needs, powerful hormones fill your body to encourage bonding, and these actually prevent you from seeing your partner's flaws. Your body is bursting with lovely endorphins that make you feel great and possibly a little bit bonkers, as you can't get enough of the person or think about anything else. If you felt like that all the time, you'd never get anything done.

Couples often feel their relationship changes when they move in together, as feeling more settled makes the hormones less necessary – they've done their job. Now you get to know the person better and have new tasks, such as adjusting to one another and building a family, that don't go with feeling high the whole time. So don't worry that the honeymoon period is over – it's a sign that the relationship is progressing.

We don't have sex

There are sometimes periods in a relationship when sex seems to have just slipped away or is too much effort. This often happens when life is especially stressful and tiring, sometimes triggered by particular life events, and usually making it awkward to get started again. Even when your libido seems to be on a permanent break, there are lots of ways to regain intimacy, many of them discussed later in the book. Don't rush it. Do talk about it. This is very common and doesn't usually mean the relationship is over.

My partner's abusing me

You've been experiencing physical, emotional, financial or sexual abuse.

It goes without saying that this isn't OK and you need to be safe. Consequently, it makes sense to plan your exit and to involve other people who can support you. Statistically, the chances of physical violence increase when you tell a partner you're thinking of leaving, even if this has never happened before, so it's important to have a plan that will allow you to split safely.

It's not a good idea to threaten leaving, especially if you don't mean it. Indeed, don't mention leaving at all until and unless you have a place to go and some support. Ironically, it's often the most critical partners, who belittle and devalue you and the relationship, who'll do anything to keep it going. Organisations that can help include:

- Men's Advice Line: www.mensadviceline.org.uk
- National Centre for Domestic Violence: www.ncdv.org.uk
- National Domestic Violence Helpline – 24 hour freephone: 0808 2000 247
- National Stalking Helpline: 0808 802 0300; www.stalking helpline.org
- Northern Ireland Women's Aid: www.niwaf.org
- Rights of Women: www.rightsofwomen.org.uk
- Scottish Women's Aid: www.scottishwomensaid.co.uk
- Wales Domestic Abuse Helpline: 0808 80 10 800
- Women's Aid Federation of England: www.womensaid.org.uk
- Welsh Women's Aid: www.welshwomensaid.org

When it's over

Hanging on to the idea that ending a relationship always equals failure leaves couples feeling resentful and out of control – but just being together doesn't necessarily equal success. Rather, unhappy relationships lead to the sort of ongoing stress that threatens health and can exacerbate illness. If they think about it, many people in unhappy relationships can't remember the last time they felt truly well, because emotional strain produces hormones that stress the body too. This makes it even harder to be proactive about what's happening. The longer the stress continues, the more difficult it may be to think straight or cope with a breakup. Nonetheless, many people just one day find themselves thinking that enough is enough, and are as surprised as their partner to be throwing in the towel.

Surprise endings

Even if you suddenly decide to end the relationship – perhaps even startling yourself – you'll probably have been thinking about this for quite a while. You may even have caught yourself planning – spotting a house you could live in, logging food you'll buy when you're out shopping for just yourself or feeling excited about things you'll do when you're single. Such moments can provide reassurance and hope or cause guilt and fear as they edge you towards the reality of the split. You need to remember that your partner probably hasn't been experiencing this and will need time to take in what's happening.

Blurting out that you want to end the relationship during an argument is often more a case of letting off steam than a real desire to end. Some people do it every time there's a row and then carry on as though nothing happened. Exaggeration like this means the relationship is continuously threatened, which is stressful in itself. Nevertheless, frequent threats lose currency and become ignored. It's dangerous to assume problems are resolved because they're no longer mentioned – often, this is because the other partner has just given up.

Often, an unhappy partner has been trying to persuade the other to discuss changes or attend relationship therapy, but the more content partner has dismissed this, perhaps through fear. We can be very selective about what we pay attention to and may just disregard what we don't like or what scares us. Waking up to a serious problem when it's too late to change is sometimes the result.

Breaking the news

Unless it's potentially unsafe to do so, make sure there's privacy, time and space for any conversation about ending. It's a good idea to let your partner know that you want to talk about the relationship so they're at least somewhat prepared for what may be to come. Explain what you've decided you want and what you hope will happen next, both immediately and longer term. Have a plan for the next few minutes, days and weeks. This may change, but don't just leave it to chance or you may both be wondering what to do next, whether you should stay or go. Though hurt and anger may make you both feel that being apart immediately is for the best, you'll need to talk about what's happened and why, and agree the details of the split.

Unless staying in your home has the potential to be dangerous, give your partner time to adjust before actually leaving. Dropping a bombshell and then clearing off may seem to provide a clean break all round, but it usually leaves the remaining partner with a mess to deal with on their own. It may be more helpful to discuss how the break can be managed together, particularly if there are children (of any age) to be told.

It's natural for your partner to want to understand what's happened and why, and to hope the relationship can be rebuilt; leaving won't prevent such thoughts. Though it may be tempting, it's important to be consistent and not to offer false hope or change an initial explanation to one that seems more acceptable, particularly if you're having to live together.

Adjusting

If you're on the receiving end, the sudden or uncontrolled ending of a relationship inevitably requires a great deal of adjustment. If you thought your relationship was sound, you may feel you just don't know your partner. Consequently, disbelief may be the major emotion for quite some time. Your priority will be to take care of yourself, avoiding rash decisions or behaviours you may regret. Let the news sink in, wait for the dust to settle and reassess your position.

Sometimes, however much you've dreaded it, there may be relief once the decision has finally been made. During this period, relationships often improve, though this thawing of relations can offer unjustified optimism. However, this needn't be a reason to maintain frostiness. Being clear and respectful about what you each want and need going forward, it's possible to create helpful boundaries and signposts that make it easier to co-operate. This can't always be achieved – there may just not be the communication tools needed to see past the red mist.

Though many of us imagine that infidelity is the main cause of breakups, poor communication is actually the most commonly cited reason couples give for relationship problems. Unfortunately, some couples' attempts to communicate well, support one another and be more than just civil during the separation process meets with the bafflement or disapproval of family and friends. When they see you co-operating, some think all the relationship needs is a bit more effort. This is a shame, as it can lead to partners who could have parted as friends creating conflict simply to justify moving on. It's hard to know how to behave, and it's likely that feelings will change from one moment to the next. Take care of yourselves and do what feels right for you, not what other people think you should do.

When there's an affair

Splitting when an affair is involved can be especially difficult. Though choosing an affair over an existing relationship may not have been easy, partners may see it as a casual decision which they can't understand. It's common to feel compelled to search for more information, whether you find out about your partner's affair by accident or because they tell you. It's almost impossible not to torture yourself by seeking detail and evidence, though it rarely helps. Obsession with your partner's behaviour and movements may fill the time while you wait for the world to turn the right way up again, turning you into someone you don't recognise or particularly like, as you check pockets, phones and e-mails, doing everything you can to catch your partner out.

This can be incredibly lonely. If you're hoping the relationship can be salvaged, you may not want to confide in friends and family in case it changes their view of your partner forever or because you feel ashamed of being let down in this way. At extremes, some people withdraw, believing their partner wouldn't have let them down if they'd been 'good enough'. Others are quick to expose what happened, shame and berate their partner. We all have different ways of coping. However, shutting down and publicly sounding off are particularly unhelpful as they don't deal with what's happened or offer a way forward. Both can be a way of denying the reality of the situation.

Sometimes an affair is a (terrible) way to end a relationship. However painful, it's less hurtful and complicated in the long run to just be honest with your partner about what you're feeling, even if you're just feeling confused. It's also important for you both to take responsibility for the state of the relationship, rather than blaming each other or yourselves exclusively or involving other people.

Feelings of betrayal can quickly turn to anger and revenge, but acting on them is unlikely to improve the situation. It's also rarely helpful to confront the person the affair was with, though it may feel much more comfortable to blame them than to explore what's happening between yourself and your partner. Rash actions and reluctance to reflect are likely to close down the possibility of either reconciliation or future friendship. Though it has to be accepted that sometimes there's just no going back, it's often possible to rebuild trust and emerge with a much better relationship if you both want to. Many couples emerge stronger together post-affair.

Telling children

Children also deserve a considered explanation of what's going on. Ideally, you'll tell them together when you both know what's going to happen, so you can reassure them about details such as where they'll live, go to school, whether they can keep friends and pets, who they'll still see. Children often adjust well if they're kept informed and both parents appear to be getting on. Adults confiding in them, complaining to them or arguing with each other cause the most distress.

Adult children also need consideration. Though some take the news in their stride, others experience great distress, especially if the split comes unexpectedly. Sometimes parents conceal their problems, so children come home from university or living away to discover the family home has been sold and one of their parents has gone. As well as being a terrible shock, this gives the impression that relationships fall apart out of the blue, which has implications for how they approach their own relationships.

Don't expect them to take sides or to be fully understanding. Even when they've witnessed the disintegration of the relationship, and support the split, adult children also need time to adjust. Sometimes they'll be angry that you didn't split earlier and save them from living in a battle zone.

Coping in the aftermath

Whether the end of the relationship comes as a huge shock, a tortuous and drawn out refusal to let go, dawning and sad realisation, a gradual acceptance of the inevitable or a massive relief, there's no template for your reactions and it's very natural to flip-flop your way through conflicting emotions. One minute you may be enjoying happy memories, and thinking you can make this work, and the next wondering what you ever saw in your partner. You'll both have good and bad days, and it makes sense to expect nothing and be ready for anything.

The unknown can be very frightening, so you may need help to get through this extremely difficult time. If you can see each small step as a major success, the light at the end of the tunnel will get closer and you'll be encouraged to keep going. It can be difficult to imagine life separately, so it's a good idea to take each day as it comes and avoid forcing major decisions. They'll be needed, but take time to fully consider all your options. Having said this, resisting a decision that's already been made helps no one. If your partner has made up their mind that the relationship really is over, working on whether it's possible to remain friends and focusing on the positives of your life together will speed recovery much more than refusing to believe what's happening. Indeed, inflexibility and fear of change stifles relationships and often keeps couples locked in an excruciating tug of war.

You may feel overwhelmed by guilt if the break was your decision. However, appreciating when your relationship truly is preventing personal growth and potential happiness, recognising that you both need something different or ending years of deadlock is ultimately commendable. However painful, it's often much harder to embrace the mental shift necessary to change than to stay put and do nothing.

The new you

Being without a partner positions you differently, not just in relation to how others see you, but also in terms of the way you see yourself. Misgivings about your single status could cause you to rush into a new relationship without sufficiently thinking about what happened in the old one(s). Just accepting change, rather than resisting it, can be a challenge. The remainder of this book explores the difficulties we all face after leaving a relationship and considering what comes next, starting in Chapter 2 with a look at how to manage the relationship with your ex.

Remember: Successful relationships allow partners to grow and change, so that sometimes they need to move on.

Bibliography

Goodman, A. and Greaves, E. (2010) *Cohabitation, Marriage and Relationship Stability*, Institute of Fiscal Studies Briefing Note BN107, London: Nuffield. www.ifs.org.uk/bns/bn107.pdf. Accessed 10 January 2017.

Chapter 2

You and your ex

Once you've made up your mind to split there's an unsettled transition period, during and after which you and your ex will need to negotiate your ongoing relationship. Separating couples are notoriously poor at explaining what they're experiencing, assuming – sometimes rightly – that their ex isn't interested. However, there's much to be gained from being clear about the relationship you want in future and keeping one another updated if you change your mind. Ideas about how you want your relationship to be will inevitably evolve as you navigate the separation process.

Unless you've been together for a very short time, it may be difficult to completely untether yourselves. Even if you have no children, most couples have many shared connections that make it difficult to cut ties completely. If you do have children, you'll have to find a way to get on well enough to co-parent and be in the same place if, in the future, you're both to be present at important events such as school plays and sports days, graduations, weddings, christenings and so on. This may mean experiencing a different kind of ending from the one you imagined, one where the relationship changes and is more distant but may still be very significant.

Engaging with change

This transition could be argued to last indefinitely, as there's unlikely to be a particular moment when you can say you've moved on. There's more likely to be a gradual realisation that you're living a different life and, perhaps, that some major issues have been resolved. However, a comfortable relationship with your ex probably isn't possible if you don't engage with change. Wanting life to stay the same or trying to resist the powerful emotions you may be feeling stalls recovery. Staying connected with a single aspect of these feelings – often anger – may seem to offer the best hope for feeling better, but actually just prolongs the pain.

It's important to realise that some grief is unavoidable when a relationship ends, even if this was your choice. It's completely normal to feel sad, worry that you could have done something differently, to avoid situations that trigger painful thoughts, to experience anxiety and depression and to sometimes feel hopeless. Sleepless nights, intrusive thoughts and even just feeling generally run-down and unwell are all common. As a distraction from all of these, some people become focused on the idea that the relationship can be recovered. At some point, though, you'll have to start recovering your life.

People often start to feel better sooner than they expected, particularly if they're able to find some positives about their new life. In other words, your attitude will make a huge difference. If you've had a terrible time, and the situation you find yourself in is hugely unfair, it's tempting to give in to bitterness. Yet, after all you've been through, you deserve to make the most of your life. If it's at all possible, take the attention off your partner and concentrate on yourself.

Enjoy doing things your way. How do you feel about reminders of your ex? It can be hugely unhelpful when separating to see your ex-partner's coat hanging in the hall every day or their favourite mug in the kitchen cupboard. If you're bereaved, however, such reminders may be of great comfort. You need to do what feels right for you, and avoid torturing yourself to achieve what you feel *ought* to be happening.

People talk in terms of 'getting over' separation and divorce, 'moving on' and 'recovering', but it has to be acknowledged that the process is both life-changing and can change your view of the life you've had. If your partner was there during another particularly stressful or joyful part of your life, for instance, you may feel as though this event changes in your memory when you split. If you've been together for many years, with a clear plan for your joint future, you may have absolutely no idea what's next and feel hugely cheated.

If your family or friends disapproved, or if it was a first or significant LGB or trans relationship, your confidence may be particularly shaken, especially if you think others have been waiting for the relationship to fail. You have to keep remembering that each relationship in your life is an important stepping stone, valid in its own right, and it's your view of it that matters, not other people's judgement. Lots of reflection and distance is needed to develop meaning and coherence about what's happened and place it within the story of your life, so take your time.

Bereavement

This is equally true if the relationship ended due to your partner's death. Sometimes, the only way to feel you have them back at all may be to let go a little. A partner's long illness and gradual decline can leave you exhausted and isolated, with little capacity for repair. A sudden loss, through a heart attack, accident or even suicide, can leave survivors too traumatised to know how to go on, with the sense that no one understands what's been experienced.

Not allowing yourself any joy, however, and hanging on to the initial profound feelings of pain and unfairness, keep you stuck at the end of the relationship rather than able to enjoy happy memories of your time together. Talking to your partner can be very helpful. Even though they're physically absent, you can imagine their response and how things would be if they were with you. They'd probably encourage you to make the most of your life and to take opportunities that weren't possible while they were ill. Equally, don't be surprised by feelings of relief. If the relationship was difficult, or if you lost the person you first fell in love with during a long illness, you'll need time to thaw out and remember who *you* are and what *you* need.

Sometimes there may be hurt or shock at what a partner has left behind, including inadequate financial arrangements or the discovery of secrets. Both practical and emotional tasks may be reminders that the person who would previously have offered support has now gone. This is made all the more difficult if you're left with mixed feelings, which may include anger at being left or even betrayal if the death uncovers aspects of your partner's life that you weren't previously aware of.

Betrayal

Ironically, at the end of a difficult relationship, some people wonder if bereavement would have been easier, perhaps wrongly imagining that it would offer a no-strings future. This may be especially the case if the breakup followed a partner's affair or other form of 'unfaithfulness', such as the discovery of sexual addiction (see also page 157). This may leave you feeling you don't know yourself any longer, let alone your partner, and that the relationship has been a sham. Managing to take care of family or hold down a job can seem impossible, and shame can feel immense and overwhelming. The last thing you may feel able to do is reconnect with your ex in any way.

Couples who don't live together or don't have children may seem fortunate, but many feel the lack of external commotion denies the pain and loss they feel. This sense of being misunderstood or minimising of your experience can also occur when others are urging you to move on and you don't feel anywhere near ready. This encourages some people to maintain and provoke conflict with their ex, as it provides external evidence to validate the hurt. Sometimes, grief and bitterness about the loss of hopes and dreams also keeps people stuck.

Hostility

Regular outbreaks of hostility can be the result. Once set up as rivals, it can be hard for separating couples to find any way to offer each other kindness and consideration or to show the genuine underlying feelings that might stimulate the other's understanding and empathy. Sometimes every contact involves some sort of criticism or accusations, with each partner trying to gain the advantage. Couples whose relationships were characterised by conflict often find it the most difficult to change. Though they may be suffering, they often show only anger, denying other emotions such as fear, shame, vulnerability, and feelings of loss, helplessness, regret and sadness. The more they feel their behaviour may have contributed to the split, the more some people blame and retaliate.

Often, both partners feel unable to move away from defensive positions where all they expect from one another – and all they feel capable of themselves – is more pain and damage. A sad side-effect of this is that it often leads ex-partners to compete to be better parents, as if winning their children's love and approval will settle the matter of who's in the right. Of course, this can have the opposite effect, pulling children in different directions and confusing them about loyalty and their own feelings of love and loss.

Managing hostility

Feeling helpless in the face of overwhelming circumstances is another reason ex-couples are so ready to blame and retaliate. If reflecting on this together is possible, you may be able to offer each other considerable support in confronting situations you both find intimidating. Even if you don't agree with the other, it can be useful to acknowledge that you're hearing what's been said and that you're aware of any distress a situation is causing. Don't necessarily respond to accusations that you haven't tried hard enough, especially if you feel you've done as much as you can. Acknowledge your ex's problem, but explain clearly why what they want isn't possible. This is more likely to result in a helpful compromise than a knee-jerk dismissal of the request or just giving in.

Listening to and respecting each other's point of view can happen in the most difficult relationships if you're able to think of complaints differently. Trying to phrase your own needs in a less blaming way is obviously helpful. Trying to imagine what's behind a criticism can also be useful. Is your ex really being difficult or are they unsure of how to behave or finding *you* awkward or unkind? Similarly, could you approach your ex's criticism in a different way? Would it work to ask what would be more helpful, for instance? Even if your ex really is being obstructive, stick to your own cool and co-operative plan. Some people can be unco-operative as a way of expressing their pain.

Calm communication

Even if you can't stand your ex, it's in your interests to do your best to at least try to be civil. If it's your ex who can't do this, it's still worth trying to stay calm and not becoming drawn into retaliatory behaviours if it is at all possible. Your composed and rational demeanour will take the fun out of winding you up and may even make your ex realise that there's much to be gained from co-operating. Some couples develop a sense of humour about the split, and many find themselves more able to offer genuine affection only once the split is happening.

Calm communication is obviously easier said than done, but is made more possible if you consider your behaviour in advance and try not to let emotions run away with you. Decide what you need from any encounter and aim for this rather than becoming side-tracked. Always try to have something pleasant to look forward to after being in touch and, ideally, a way of downloading your experience. Don't forget that you can call Samaritans (0845 7909 090) if you need someone to talk to. Couple counselling can be useful even when there's no chance of going back, so that you both feel you've given voice to your experience and can develop a plan and some guidelines for going forward.

When you're separating or newly separated may not seem the time for an objective appraisal of your past and future relationship, but this can have a profound effect on your children. Adult children can experience surprisingly intense emotional reactions to their parents' separation, while younger children's whole view of the world can be affected by what they see and experience growing up. Your relationship becomes the model for their own, and may cause them to make similar mistakes and adopt similarly unhelpful attitudes – or the reverse, if you're able to show them a mature approach. If it's difficult to look at your own relationship objectively, it can be helpful to consider the way your own parents related, the effect this had on you and what they could have done differently.

Do spend time imagining and thinking through how you want the relationship to be and seeing how much this agrees with what your partner wants. There may even be ways you can help each other to achieve and maintain the desired contact, but only if you're clear about what's possible. You'll need to update this as time passes too, as circumstances change and your needs alter accordingly.

Reminders

For those who do manage to get on, a responsible approach to separation sometimes fails because you're both touchingly reminded of what worked for you. This can evoke guilt and sadness about the split, which may even draw you together again – only to create more regret and heartache when the reunion doesn't work. As we learned in Chapter 1, it's often easier to maintain a frosty distance, or even to provoke conflict, to get through this. Ultimately, though, it's important to remember that you're getting on because you're apart, not because you should be together. Count your blessings that you can maintain a workable relationship.

Even when you've made a clean or cleanish break, news of your partner or unexpected memories can have a surprisingly powerful effect. Obsessive checking of social media can create problems too, especially when this is how you learn unexpected or unwelcome news. Sometimes social media can make the breakup particularly public. It may be that well-meaning friends openly offer their opinion or advice, or that you and your partner use a public forum for revenge. If you don't want to risk this sort of contact with your ex, delete their details from your devices and apps. You may need contact details in case of issues with the children, for instance, but you don't need to be following their progress on Instagram. Similarly, you don't want to live your future life hoping they'll see from your online presence how well (or not) you're doing. Neither way can you actually be yourself, or discover what sort of genuine relationship you can have if you're in touch at all.

If you have an ex who won't let go, it may be wise to suggest a period of time without contact to allow them to adjust. This may seem heartless, but you can't be responsible for their emotional wellbeing, and you each need to find ways to move on and take care of yourselves. Indeed, for most separating couples, a period with drastically reduced contact provides time to adjust to life without the other. This space can help put doubts to rest, and it may come as a huge relief if you've been struggling with having to continue living together.

Dos and don'ts

Once apart, put in place some agreements about what sort of contact is acceptable and how often. For instance, daily check-ins are probably a bit much, whereas a weekly catch-up about the family may be acceptable if you get along well and this doesn't feel intrusive. You need clear rules about coming in and out of the house if one of you is living in the family home (it's generally not on – call first and make sure the door key is returned). Think through how you want to be when dropping off pets or children too. Do you stay and have a drink together? Is that OK sometimes and not others – if one of you is too busy, for instance, or if a new partner is in the house or waiting for you? Discussing these issues ahead of time may seem uncomfortable, but actually saves awkwardness in the long run.

Initially, it's probably helpful to only meet up with your ex if there's a good reason to do so. Otherwise, you may begin to depend on their company and miss other social opportunities or delay accepting the relationship is really over. If you suggest meeting, be clear about the purpose to avoid offering false hope or appearing to want a date. If meeting with your ex is essential, but is painful or triggers anxiety, try to have other people around to distract you and offer support. If you're getting on with your ex during this period, it can be easy to misread signals, or think it's worth having another go at the relationship, and then finding yourself back in the emotional place you'd started to get over. Alternatively, you may feel another go is worth a try and push your ex to the point where they feel no contact at all is the best option. Don't stalk them, have sex with them, put provocative posts on social media, take revenge or complain about them endlessly.

Be aware that some relationships with friends and family may need renegotiating too. For example, it can be very hard to lose your ex's family if you got on well, particularly if they continue to want a relationship with your children but not with you. Grumbling about your ex to them won't make it easier to stay in touch either. Even if they were to agree with you, loyalty or avoidance of conflict may prevent them from admitting this. However, even if they want to see you as much as ever, do consider how your ex may feel about this. Until a new equilibrium has been established, also think carefully before accepting invitations for big family events. Find ways to create a new life for yourself that doesn't depend entirely on your ex and their family.

New partners

The appearance of a new partner can be more painful than you'd imagined, especially if they're welcomed by your ex's family or your joint friends. This may make a difference to how often you see your ex or the arrangements you've made since the split. You and the new partner may each feel threatened by the other, even when you instigated the breakup.

Try especially hard to avoid hostility if your children will be spending time with the new partner. It's in everyone's interests if you all get on. They're more likely to agree with your requests and wishes if you do, and your children are less likely to be upset. Remember that they aren't there to fight your battles, spy or pass messages back and forth, and that you'll want the same respect for your new partner too when you have one.

Though it's important to take into account the wishes of new partners, they also need to understand the importance of friendly contact with *your* ex, especially if children are involved or there's any chance of you all having to be together at family events. If either one of you needs reassurance about the relationship with exes, do ask for it rather than being angry or taking it out on the ex. If you're on the receiving end of a new partner's anger, on the other hand, bear in mind that it may be easier for them to blame any of their relationship problems on you than on your ex. You may actually have a great deal in common.

It may be a good idea to have some plans for the day if your ex marries their new partner. Your children will probably go to the wedding, so you'll have to think of something else to keep you occupied. Try to make this as celebratory as possible. You can see it as the proper beginning of *your* new life as well as your ex's, so try to start it as you mean to go on.

Changes in your ex

Do be aware that both of you will change as a result of the split. It can be annoying if your ex now appears to have taken on board what you've been telling them for years, and has made changes in the new relationship that they didn't make for you. However, it may have taken your split for them to wake up to the need to change if they were ever to make a relationship work.

There are times when partners deliberately continue abusing you by suggesting that their new love is so perfect that they changed for them. If you were in an abusive relationship before, realise that safety should still be your main concern. Try not to see your ex alone and prioritise your own needs rather than being coerced into anything that doesn't seem 100 per cent reasonable and agreeable to you. Sticking to any agreements you've made is important to establish clear boundaries and dissuade your ex from thinking you can be bullied. Address any problems as soon as possible, in the presence of other people if you fear confrontation. If you feel in any way threatened, seek help, calling the police if necessary. Feeling separate and able to manage your ex will become easier as you get used to the new you, the subject of Chapter 3.

Remember: Being open to change while prioritising your own needs will help you through this uncertain period when you are likely to experience a wide variety of, possibly conflicting, emotions.

Chapter 3

Your single self

Negative expectations about how life will be after a relationship breakup inevitably affect confidence and hope. If you're feeling battered by the split, you probably just want to know how soon you'll feel anything like normal. How long it takes to start feeling better will be influenced by how you feel life treated you before and whether you have experience of overcoming difficulties successfully. How able you are to seek and accept the practical and emotional support you need may also influence your progress, and there are some gender differences.

Men are often assumed to be less able to care for themselves, so people rally round them, offering distraction and practical support. Women often find this hugely unfair, especially when they feel they're the one struggling. However, possibly because men are more socialised not to express their feelings, they're sometimes less able to create a coherent narrative about what's happened. A 2015 study of nearly 6,000 men in 19 countries concluded that, although they often start out feeling positive after a breakup, men's distress may be more prolonged. Meanwhile, women – who are, incidentally, more likely to initiate a separation – recover from early feelings of powerlessness and bleakness, and often emerge feeling more in control of their lives. They're more likely to work at making sense of the split and to process their thoughts and feelings through talking.

Re-evaluating relationships

Knowing who to confide in and what or how much to tell can be tricky though. You may feel you need to review your relationships with your family, friends and especially your children, who may be particularly inappropriate confidantes. It's not always easy to know who is innocently passing private information to your ex or who really doesn't want to talk about the split. Sometimes, mutual friends and your ex's family either don't want to get involved or side with your ex. Whether or not this is expected, it's natural to feel disappointed and hurt, but your ex's family and friends may feel more able to engage with you once some time has passed and the dust has settled.

Although it can be a shock to realise that friends aren't rallying round quite as much as you expected, make the most of those who do want to be helpful and don't let those who are less forthcoming drift away altogether. In particular, don't automatically ditch people you feel you can't confide in. They may not be good at the serious stuff but great for some fun when you're feeling up to it. Some people are nervous about friends who separate, as it triggers fears about *their* relationship and how they would cope on their own. Similarly, some people who aren't happy in their relationship are reminded that they should really tackle this, and feel judged or weak for not being brave enough to do so. Some people are just poor at giving support. They may be great mates when all is well but rubbish at listening or giving advice. This may especially be the case if they feel required to take sides. If possible, show that this isn't necessary and that you still want to be friends even if they like your partner too. If you feel unable to let go of anger and pain, it's possible that those around you *will* be frightened off. Remember, no one has an obligation to be there for you – they choose to because they care – nor is it your role to judge and find others lacking if not all your needs are met.

It's not necessary to have a continuously happy face, but there does come a point when others have heard your story many times and don't know what to say next. Vary what you tell them a bit and try to begin with something positive when asked how you are. Don't be tempted to confide in your children about your ex's shortcomings. Bear in mind that they're the same flesh and blood, so this may affect how they feel about themselves. It may also damage their relationship with that parent, and potentially with you.

Bin preconceived ideas

In among the people you know, there will undoubtedly be some who surprise you with their sympathy and concern. Often, the trick to feeling supported is to bin your preconceived ideas of what this will look like and be open to the different ways others offer care. For instance, you may expect regular or daily phone calls from a close friend who doesn't realise this and feels it's more appropriate to take you for a long chat over coffee or a beer once a fortnight. Indeed, it's when you emerge from a long relationship that you may first begin to notice how different we all are and how there's little that can be taken for granted. This need to understand the different meanings that people attribute to events and ideas will always have been there, but it sometimes takes a big change to make us notice. Even in conflictual relationships, where hostility can reinforce personal beliefs on both sides, each of you may have made assumptions about what the other meant. Not wondering about meaning can be a downfall of companionable relationships, as neither of you considers you may be misreading the other.

Starting to notice a 'changed world' can be highly unsettling, especially if you're wondering about the way you appear to other people. If you've spent decades living with someone else, considering their needs, relating to them, and just knowing they're there, of course finding yourself alone will need some adjustment. Even a short relationship can leave you missing someone. Day-to-day activities may also have altered dramatically if you've had to change or find a job, move house, do more or less childcare, spend more time alone or in company, have more or less money or control of your finances. You may become a single parent, a lone tenant – you will be, and you will have, an ex.

Your split has implications for, and repositions, other people too. Your family and friends, for example, may not know whether to stay in touch with your ex or how they should behave with them if they do. Indeed, friendships may be affected in both practical and emotional ways. You might not be able to afford nights out with your friends. They may not invite you round or out so often if they're trying to balance how often they see you and your ex. They may even try to set you up with a new partner.

Your children will also be juggling their relationships with both of you and may be worried about what their future holds, especially in terms of getting to know a new partner or step-siblings. You may also no longer be able to offer childcare for your grandchildren if you now have to work or move away.

Should you date?

A study of students at Monmouth University, New Jersey, determined that it takes from three to 18 months to 'get over' even a short relationship, though it isn't clear whether dating before this is helpful. A deep reluctance to risk loss again discourages some people from becoming close to anyone, particularly following a partner's death. Others want to pick up their lives and savour every moment with or without a new partner. Still others long for a new relationship at once, especially if there are no issues with the partner they've lost. Some men, in particular, wish to replace a happy relationship as soon as possible, even after a bereavement. This is often because they've already found a place for the lost partner in their hearts and are able to comfortably go forward with no doubts. As far as they're concerned, their forever relationship with their lost partner is as strong as it could possibly be and they know that nothing will ever threaten that, no matter how important other events and relationships become.

Alternatively, some people find it so hard to cope with their loss, or feel so strongly that they shouldn't show the world their true feelings, that they seek a new relationship long before they're truly ready. Family and friends often have a view about when or whether a new relationship is a good idea and gloss over confidence and trust issues that may be very real barriers to starting again. What you want to do and what you feel is expected of you may be confusing. Pay attention to how you feel, what feels right for you and what's possible in your circumstances.

You may feel your changed body or emotional wounds leave you ill-equipped, or you may even believe you never knew how to get relationships right in the first place. It's certainly helpful to allow time to settle into being your new single self. How your life will develop is yet to be discovered. This uncertainty may feel anything from bleak to exciting, but forcing yourself to start behaving in ways that don't feel comfortable won't help you to learn how you want your new life to be.

As time passes, a new relationship may seem less appealing than expected, more difficult to find, harder to manage or so thrilling that it's overwhelming. The longer the previous relationship, the more likely it is that you'll find you've changed and that what you thought you wanted no longer works. Many of us also feel differently positioned when we're single. There may be negative beliefs about self-worth or shame about being alone that stops you from considering another relationship or causes you to seek one, whatever its quality. The status you feel is associated with having a partner may be what drives you to find one, even if you're perfectly happy single.

Creating and coming to terms with a new self-image is essential to comfortably moving on. Some people feel completely differently about their sexuality and may, for instance, be interested in exploring same-sex experiences without any idea how to go about this. Some people may be surprised to find they prefer to be alone or to keep relationships casual. Some may have tried dating and felt it was a disaster, losing hope that they'll ever find love, or even a pleasant evening out.

Embracing positives

You may grow through many different stages, feeling completely differently at different times, or you may feel you've flatlined, experiencing nothing but numbness. Whether you feel any better as time passes depends very much on how able you are to see the positives in your situation. You can't be expected to leap for joy and embrace the future wholeheartedly if your new life is not what you chose. Even if it is, you may have doubts about whether you've done the right thing – or even what that might be – or fears about whether you'll be able to manage by yourself. You may feel guilt or distress are appropriate for the time being or even be reluctant to feel better in case your ex and others minimise the ongoing effect of the split.

However, research suggests that the ability to find some sort of positive in a difficult situation helps people to cope. For instance, having time to yourself while your partner has the children may give you previously unknown freedom to pursue your own interests. Even if your relationship had no difficulties, you'll almost certainly have been restricted in some activities or preferences just because people who live together are forced to compromise. Now's your chance to eat what you want, watch what you like, go where you choose, see who you prefer and try new activities, places and possibilities.

Fake it 'til you make it

The idea that looking for positives makes you feel better actually has a scientific basis, whereas constantly talking about a breakup just makes us glum. This isn't at all to say you shouldn't express how you're feeling, but you could experiment with the idea of pretending you feel better. This pretence is absolutely not meant to fool the world or put on a brave face for the sake of other people. It's more of an investigation to try out what it might be like to feel different and what it might take to achieve that. Sometimes it can help to imagine how someone you admire would cope in your situation. This can be anyone from a friend or relative, famous celebrity, to a historical or fictitious character. Pretending you're them or doing what they'd do gives you a chance to try on a different way to be.

Other experiments might include having people over for a meal, accepting an invitation, going on holiday, learning something new – only you know what might be fun or useful. Many people find it helps to keep a journal of their feelings and progress, and to set themselves goals as experiments which they log. By doing this, you're able to see how much you've achieved, which instils hope and positivity. Of course, one experiment you could try would be to go on a date. First, though, you'll have to find someone to go out with.

Online dating

To start looking, computer skills will come in handy, as online dating is fast becoming *the* way for couples to meet, with the biggest rise in online dating in the 55–64 age group. According to dating website eHarmony, half of all couple relationships will begin online within 20 years and, by 2040, 70 per cent of relationships will have involved technology. Not all older online users are looking for love, of course, and many make up for lost time with casual sexual relationships, friends with benefits or just friends. To meet people quickly, there are apps like Tinder (straight) and Grindr (gay) which display available people in your area. You simply swipe your phone screen to indicate interest. If that person is interested too, you could be meeting in no time. However, most online relationships take a bit more work.

Getting started online

You may feel wary about the whole idea of online dating, and it's absolutely sensible to be cautious; after all, you're contacting a complete stranger. Websites on how to use online dating sites safely and successfully have burgeoned in response, advising not just about which site to choose, the language to use and how to create an online profile, but also warning about scammers and predators. However, it's not the safety aspect that usually seems daunting. While it's been estimated that three-quarters of millennials have used dating apps or websites, many older people worry that they ought to be able to meet someone 'naturally'. Though it's diminishing, some stigma remains, with nearly a quarter of Americans polled by the Pew Research Center associating online dating with 'desperation' (Smith and Anderson, 2016). Nonetheless, many of the steeply climbing number who favour meeting online believe they'll learn considerably more about their dates this way. This may feel safer than, say, meeting in a bar. Some online 'daters' never actually meet but thoroughly enjoy chatting.

You'll probably know a few people who have started relationships online – indeed, they may have been encouraging you to try online dating – so pick their brains and let them help you get started. Be aware that you'll need to make time for this. Have a really good look at as many of the online dating sites as you can to get an idea of what's out there, the kind of profile that seems attractive and also the sort of site that's more likely to suit you. Some are devoted to matching people according to hobbies or interests, and there are even sites matching people according to shared dislikes.

Some people use more than one website and check them all every day. If you're short of time, late afternoon on a Sunday or 3pm on Tuesdays is meant to be when your chances of finding matches are maximised! When you're looking for a date, try to keep an open mind. The more you find out about someone, the more you may like them. On the other hand, also decide what would be a deal-breaker for you. For instance, if you're looking for love or friendship, don't agree to meet someone wildly attractive whose beliefs and attitudes you find abhorrent. If you're after a casual/physical relationship, however, your date's outlook may be irrelevant. Though you may be asked what sort of person you're looking for, don't make too many demands. Not only does it limit your choice, but you'll either come across as super picky or downright unrealistic.

Your profile

You'll have to write a profile that 'sells' you quickly, and you'll need to include at least one photograph. Make these as realistic as possible. You'll want your date to recognise you when you meet and not to be disappointed! Use recent photographs of yourself, smiling.

You can't please all of the people all of the time, but you can try not to put people off unnecessarily. For instance, don't put up a picture of yourself with a fast car (especially if it's not yours), hoping to be seen as successful and exciting, unless you're also happy to be considered a flashy show-off. In other words, realise that the message people receive may not always be the one you intended.

Remember that whoever sees your post may be glancing through a great number very quickly and probably won't be pausing to consider whether you're sending nuanced messages. However, being eye-catching isn't such a good idea if it's for the wrong reasons. A provocative pose or outfit could give the impression you just want sex, not a relationship, for example. No one will know if what you actually mean is: *Look what fun I can be. If I like you and we become close, I can be a caring and skilled lover.* If no-strings sex is what you want, saying you're into no-strings fun will do the trick, but don't expect people who want a more serious relationship to be in touch too. However, if you're looking for an outdoorsy person, pictures of you camping or skiing probably will attract someone with similar interests. Posting more than one picture makes you seem more open, and changing your profile picture regularly may make others look again or think you're a new user.

The profile you write needs some consideration. Again, you don't want to be off-putting, but neither do you want to seem bland. Study other profiles to see what appeals to you. This isn't the time to be too modest, but try not to sound arrogant. You'll need to appear confident and be prepared to promote yourself, but resist the temptation to show off: 'I like to keep fit' sounds better than, 'You won't believe my super toned body'. Give information on a need-to-know basis. Giving a mobile number or e-mail address makes it harder for anyone to trace you, whereas your full name, home address and landline number could lead to someone turning up. Many people these days have a considerable online presence, making them relatively easy to find offline too, so an abbreviated name or nickname will help you to stay in control of when you meet and how findable you are. Similarly, keep your baggage in your bag. Potential dates probably don't want to know what a hard time you've been having. Telling the world that you've survived a terrible divorce, just been made bankrupt, recovered from a serious illness or bereavement or, worse, that you're looking for someone to help you through these tough times, isn't likely to attract interest. You may be keen to celebrate surviving life's adversities – indeed, online dating may be your way of doing so – but others aren't to know that you don't *just* want someone to look after you. It's important to share these issues once you start becoming close, but realise they may not appeal to anyone coming across your online details.

Dos and don'ts of first contact

Once online, don't just sit back and wait for someone to contact you – the idea is to message people you like the look of.

- Don't feel you can only message or arrange to meet one person at a time. This won't be expected, even if you agree to a second date.
- Do be as proactive as you can and don't expect answers to every message.
- Don't feel you have to bother replying to someone you really don't warm to.
- Don't send exactly the same message to everyone.
- Do make your initial communication positive and personal if you can, perhaps mentioning some information from the person's profile.
- Do feel you can say what attracts you to them, but don't send sexually explicit messages.
- Do decide how far you're prepared to travel before you contact anyone, and stick to that decision for as long as possible.
- Don't be too tempted to travel far and wide if you don't hear from anyone initially. Unless you're free to dash about all over the place, it may be better to tweak your profile or find a new photograph before extending your search area. Getting to know someone in a different town may be attractive if you're worried about bumping into them at the supermarket but, if the relationship takes off, a long journey to meet may become tiresome. On the other hand, don't miss out on the love of your life for the sake of a few miles.

Caution

Opinions vary about how much time you should spend getting to know someone before you arrange a meeting. Some advice is to spend as much time as possible bonding with the person by messaging, while others caution against the pseudo-intimacy this can create. It could also be dispiriting to invest weeks of your time only to find the person creepy or offensive when you actually speak. So, after a couple of messages, it may be helpful to progress to telephone calls or, better still, video messaging. You'll be more able to know who to look out for if you do meet, and may be more relaxed about the meeting. You'll also know that you're talking to a real person. There are some sophisticated scams where you could be enticed into an online relationship and then bitten for cash or credit card details. The 'date' appears to have a genuine online presence, and seems solvent, but any photos of the person you've seen won't be real. Be especially wary if they start talking about a future together or marriage, or if they start sending sexually explicit messages or photos unbidden – you're being reeled in.

Most online daters aren't scammers. However, don't feel you have to continue contact if you're sure the person's not for you. But don't give up too soon either. A great deal is written online about 'the Spark', that mutual sense of attraction we all seem to believe is necessary for relationships to work. But sometimes it takes a while to feel 'the Spark', or else your friendship just grows slowly into something more solid. Many experienced daters warn that initial very bright Sparks often just as quickly fizzle out.

Preparation

Arranging just to go for a coffee or drink for your first meeting means you won't be stuck with someone all evening or have to pay for an expensive dinner if you don't hit it off. Dress for the occasion – leave the tiara or tuxedo at home if you're just meeting for a coffee. Tell someone where you're going and give them the details of the person you're meeting.

Don't give out more than your mobile number and e-mail address to the date just yet, and arrange to meet in a public place. Ideally, make that somewhere you know so that you won't get lost on the way. Even if you haven't been there before, don't let your date pick you up from home or drop you off. These days you can check out venues online and be sure the place isn't in the back of beyond or inaccessible by public transport. If you're at all worried, arrange in advance for a cab to pick you up afterwards as well as take you there. Having a cab waiting also means the date can end without awkwardness. Make sure you take enough money for transport and expect to split the bill. If discussing money makes you uncomfortable, address this before the date or early on when you meet.

The date

You should have plenty to talk about. You may not if one of you is very shy or desperate not to make a fool of themselves. If this is you, explain that you're nervous – but don't reveal too much too soon. For instance, if anxiety gives you tummy trouble, don't let on. Don't talk about your ex or the abysmal time you've been going through. Bare facts (you're divorced, single or widowed) are often enough at this stage, and emotion can come later. However, do ask questions and express interest. If your views don't coincide, don't be rude about this; you don't need to see the person again. Speaking of rudeness, put away your phone – you don't want your companion to think you're arranging your next date while you're still on this one.

Don't expect perfection or be disappointed if the date isn't as wonderful as you were hoping. Your date may just be anxious and tongue-tied or seem overconfident through nerves. However, if the date isn't going well, and you're sure you won't want to meet again, don't feel you have to stay. This is just wasting your time, so do feel you can leave when you're ready.

Even if the date does go brilliantly from your point of view, be realistic about your expectations for the future. There'll be lots of frogs before you find your prince or princess and, knowing this, your date may have other people to see as well as you. Some people just search for one date at a time, while others employ a scatter-bomb approach. Consequently, a date that goes well sometimes isn't followed up immediately, but the person gets in touch again later when they've seen some other people too. This may feel insulting, but try to be as light-hearted as you can. If someone wants to see you again, don't reject them just because they didn't come back to you quickly enough.

Afterwards, don't play hard to get. If you like the person, let them know. Keep in mind that they can soon go back online to search again if you seem to be a non-starter. While you're elusively waiting around for a second text or call, your date may have moved on. If you don't respond straight away, they may assume your meeting didn't go as well for you as they'd thought. It's likely that many dates won't work out, and online daters get used to picking themselves up and moving on, not hanging around and moping or playing games.

Dating etiquette

You've probably heard about the nasty practice of *ghosting* – deleting all online links to a person and disappearing without any explanation. Don't do this, and don't try to contact someone who does it. They aren't worth it.

Don't make assumptions about sexual expectations or let what you believe to be expected put you off. Now more than ever, there are no rules about when your relationship should become sexual or what that means. What's more important is how you feel. You may feel you deserve to let loose your sexuality and to have lots of casual sexual relationships, feel you want to keep sex for someone special or have an open mind about what might happen. The really important issue is to be safe. It's all too easy to feel amorous after a few drinks and to find yourself alone with someone you barely know without your wits about you. The chances are that this will result in nothing but a fun night, but there's a small risk you could end up, say, being robbed or sexually assaulted.

Knowing the risks and planning appropriately offers peace of mind and fewer unwelcome surprises. For instance, despite considerable publicity about the risks, there's been a massive increase in sexually transmitted diseases (STDs) in the over-fifties, mainly due to the number of straight older adults rejoining the world of dating without a clue about the dangers of unprotected sex or the symptoms of sexually transmitted infection. Postmenopausal women are less likely to use condoms once they can't conceive, but may be more likely to acquire STDs due to thinning of the vaginal wall. And drugs like Viagra have given more men confidence to engage in sex with multiple partners. So, if there is even a remote chance that you may engage in sexual activity, it's sensible to carry condoms. Seek medical advice if you have any unusual itching, bleeding, genital lumps, bumps, skin lesions or discharge after sex. Some sexually transmitted infections have no symptoms or appear to go away if you leave them, but may still be active or dormant in your body, so you must get them treated. The NHS Choices website has advice and information about where to go for help (www.nhs.uk/Livewell/Talkingaboutsex/Pages/Ineedhelpnow.aspx).

Rekindling old flames

Now that we're all more likely to be in touch via social media, many people find themselves reconnecting with old flames when they become single or when a relationship becomes dull or problematic. Sometimes these reconnections blossom into beautiful relationships, but it's important to remember this person is your ex for a reason, and to proceed with caution. If they go back a long way, they also probably know a lot about you. This can be very comforting, but it can also mean they don't appreciate the ways in which you've moved on. They may also reconnect you with a whole lot of baggage from your past that you'd prefer forgotten.

Similarly, people who've been around for years as friends are seen differently when you're single. The big issue with them as potential partners is that they'll have known both you and your ex, who may not respond well to news that you're now dating their best mate. Family – especially your children – and friends may have a negative view about what you're doing too, meaning that the relationship either begins in secrecy or without the support of those close to you. If it's at all possible, it's important not to lose touch with important others. While your new partner may feel like the most important person in the world right now, recognise that living in a bubble for two puts an incredible strain on relationships, offering nowhere to turn if anything goes wrong. It isn't just that the relationship may not work out; if one or both of you were to become ill, for instance, you might really need your family and friends.

Family and friends sometimes express concerns at the outset of a new relationship because they care about you. If you can appreciate this, and acknowledge that you understand why they have doubts, it's easier for them to hear that you hope they're wrong and really want to give this relationship a chance. Grown-up children may fear dating means they'll be pushed out of your life, so make clear that you still want a relationship with them and are including them, even if they seem rejecting. If you keep on being there, it's much easier to reunite than if you've both spat the dummy.

Sexual identity

If you're gay or exploring a new sexual identity, you may find expressing sexuality in the way you choose is much easier than you expected, but it can be harder to meet partners. Due to the hook-up apps, it seems many gay bars and clubs have been closing, making it more difficult to just mingle and enjoy gay culture. Having said that, there are plenty of gay online dating sites and advice sites (such as www.lgbt.co.uk/community/lgbt-advice-support-groups. htm) offering really useful support and information related to gay, trans and other sexualities. There's also a large community of information about the asexualities (such as http://asexualadvice.tumblr. com) which is well worth exploring if you don't want to be involved in a conventional sexual relationship.

Katie and Jerad

Your first gay relationship, or acknowledgement of gay feelings, may be the reason for your previous relationship breakup, or it may have taken you by surprise. Either way, you may feel unreasonably responsible for the reactions of family and friends as well as dealing with your own feelings, or you may experience a great sense of liberation and non-stop celebration. Most likely, you'll flip-flop somewhere between the two extremes.

If you're older, you may anticipate less support from family and friends. However, disapproval is often more to do with supporting other people who may feel hurt than homophobia. For instance, Katie's family and friends, and some of Jerad's too, were furious with Jerad when he left Katie to live with another man after three years of marriage. Jerad had felt he was doing the right thing by Katie in not continuing to pretend he didn't have gay feelings. Katie and her friends understandably felt he should have been honest from the start, but Jerad insisted he genuinely hadn't been attracted to men when they first married. In therapy, Jerad realised that the support and care Katie offered had allowed him to acknowledge feelings he'd been trying to suppress. Ironically, it was the strength of their relationship that had allowed him to be himself.

Breakup guilt

Internalised homophobia, which may have affected you throughout your life, can be a much more real problem than other people's reactions to your changing sexuality. Worryingly, feelings of guilt and responsibility make some people give up all their rights when their straight relationship ends. However, it's important to consider your future needs and not to be panicked into making decisions that aren't in your long-term best interests, however guilty you may feel about a relationship breakup.

One issue with early gay relationships may be that of coming out. It's not uncommon for an out partner to pressure the other to discuss their sexuality with family and friends sooner than they feel able to. This is often a result of insecurity and possibly a feeling that, once out, there is no turning back, especially if you've come from a straight relationship. If you're the one pushing, do realise that if coming out goes badly, your partner could be resentful and depressed, which won't help your relationship. Friends and family may have doubts or think the gay relationship is a phase. They may also need persuading that children won't be adversely affected or that they'll be excluded from your new lifestyle. Some partners worry that they aren't 'good enough' at being gay, so new companions need to be sensitive, as it may feel easier to walk away than make mistakes.

If you do experience discrimination or have difficulties with coming out, the LGBT Foundation (www.lgbt.foundation) has a daily helpline from 10am to 10pm. The campaigning organisation Stonewall can also offer information and support (www.stonewall. org.uk/help-advice); it carried out a YouGov survey about the experience and needs of older gay people (www.stonewall.org. uk/sites/default/files/LGB_people_in_Later_Life__2011_.pdf). Pink Therapy (http://pinktherapy.mobi) can help you explore relationship issues.

Whatever your sexuality, the greatest barrier to meeting a new partner is probably not their availability but wariness. It's completely natural to feel shy about starting a new sexual relationship, especially if you've been with the same partner for a long time. However, this can seem even more difficult if you start looking for reasons why it will all go wrong, rather than being excited about using your experience and discovering lots that's new. Sometimes, for example, medical issues or personal habits that you wouldn't normally think about become hugely worrying when considered in relation to sex. Many people, for instance, have to get up for the loo several times a night, which may feel embarrassing in a new relationship. Surgery may also affect body confidence, and if you haven't had sex for years you may wonder if your body's still in working order! Sex is discussed in more detail in Chapter 11, but the best advice is to be honest about your fears and concerns. Otherwise, your partner may assume you're avoiding sex because you're not interested, rather than that it's too soon or that you feel a bit awkward or shy.

Proceed at your own pace. You'll have plenty to think about as you start your new life, and a new relationship may be low on the agenda until you feel you have more practical issues sorted out, such as where to live and who with. If you're leaving one relationship for another, you may want some time to yourself before settling with your new partner – perhaps trying to keep your children at the same school or waiting until you retire. Current constraints don't stop you planning though. Single or partnered, if you have to make an interim move, you can still check out places you might like to live and make plans for a different life. If you've always wanted a dog, for instance, now's the time to get one. If you want to live by the sea, start planning. If you like the idea of spending every Sunday walking, reading, sleeping, watching box-sets or playing games, do it. Change your hair, your tastes, what you eat, watch and wear. Or don't – working out what suits you is the key to make being single positive and rewarding.

It helps to develop a routine and to create a balance of aspects that are the same and comforting, as well as introducing some new and welcome elements to your life. You may prefer to stay close to friends and family and to continue activities you previously enjoyed – such as keeping up hobbies and meeting friends – as well as looking for new opportunities. There are some websites listed at the end of the chapter to help. See this as your chance to make constructive choices about change and to reappraise your whole outlook. Complete the questionnaire below to help you plan your new life.

Exercise: Plan your life

- How do you want to spend your time?
- What have you always wanted to do that wasn't possible before?
- What do you do that makes you feel good about yourself?
- What triggers you to feel sad, resentful or lonely?
- What do you enjoy or find fulfilling?
- What would make your life fuller?
- What could you do to feel more content?
- What goals do you have in the short, medium and longer term?
- What would tell you that you are living the life you want?
- What helps you to live the life you want?
- What is getting in the way?

- Are there any thoughts or beliefs that interfere with you achieving your goals?
- What do you need to stop doing to feel better?
- On a scale of 1–10, how far is your life the way you want it to be?
- What would help you to increase your score?

Using the questionnaire will help you begin to look at what's achievable and what's stopping you from doing what you'd like. You may want to create goals and instructions for yourself with a realistic timescale that you can review as your new life gets started. There'll be practical matters to address, but you may also want to try adjusting your attitudes and throwing away any unhelpful beliefs that are holding you back. For example, you may need to give yourself permission to be yourself and do what makes you happy, especially if you've always been used to putting other people first.

The greatest obstacle for some people is the idea that being alone automatically equals loneliness. The photograph exercise below may help you to feel less alone, demonstrating that – though life changes – we can learn from the past and the selves we've passed through. Without the past we'd have no experience to guide us. On the other hand, we can become confused by messages and beliefs about how we ought to be rather than what we can be and want to be. This exercise allows you to reconnect with your younger self and use this as a way to unravel helpful ideas from unhelpful ones, adopting a more straightforward approach going forward.

Exercise: Using your younger self

Find a photograph from any time in your childhood or adolescence. It's important that you choose the picture yourself, but it doesn't matter whether this is a portrait or there are other people in the picture. Make sure you're comfortable and have enough time and mental space for the exercise, then look at the photograph and silently find a way to greet the younger you in the picture before asking the following questions.

- What was happening on the day the picture was taken, beforehand and afterwards?
- Whose idea was it to take the picture? Do you remember being pleased or reluctant to be photographed?

- Who took the photograph? What was your relationship with them then and what is your relationship now?
- Who else is in the picture? What was the relationship with them then and what is it now?
- Who may be standing on the periphery of the picture? Why were they there?
- What else was happening in your life around the time the picture was taken?
- Thinking of the picture itself, is this one of your favourites or one you don't see often?
- Where does it normally live – on display or is it in an album or a drawer? If you don't own it, who is the keeper of the picture?
- What would the person in the picture think of where the photo is kept? Would they be pleased or annoyed?
- What would they think of you now? Would they be proud of you or ashamed of you? Would they be surprised by your life or has it turned out as they would have expected?
- If you could give them a piece of advice, what would that be?
- If they could give you some advice, what would they say?
- Continue the conversation with the person in the picture as long as you like and then find a way to say goodbye for now, letting them know when you may be speaking again.

Afterwards, think about what was happening around the time the photograph was taken. Is the young person in the photo you chose still untroubled by life's events or have they already been affected by some sort of trauma? If so, was this a turning point, when life changed? Either way, your younger self may be able to help you now. If they're as yet untroubled in life, their fresh, straightforward and innocent approach could provide just the advice you need now. If, on the other hand, they've had a difficult time, perhaps you can be reminded of how you coped then. What qualities did you use to help you then and would they be useful now? Some people manage to use their photograph to develop an ongoing dialogue with their younger self who can keep them company and help with current difficulties. Though talking to your photo may seem strange to begin with, the younger version of you could become a helpful companion, guiding you through life with wise advice and friendship.

Some of what you want to change may be your attitude to relationships. The next section looks at what happens in relationships, how experience and personality reflects that and what you could do differently next time.

Remember: Not having to consider someone else can be a luxury, so make the most of it.

Resources

Singles holidays

Just You: www.justyou.co.uk
One Traveller: www.onetraveller.co.uk
Riviera Travel: www.rivieratravel.co.uk/single-holidays
Saga Singles: http://travel.saga.co.uk/holidays/holiday-types/singles-holidays.aspx
Solos Holidays: www.solosholidays.co.uk

Education

University of the Third Age: www.u3a.org.uk
Open University: www.open.ac.uk

Fun

Meetup: www.meetup.com

Bibliography

Lewandouski, G. and Bixxoco, N. (2007) Addition through subtraction: Growth following the dissolution of low-quality relationships. *The Journal of Positive Psychology*, 21(1), 40–54.

Morris, C. E., Reiber, C. and Roman, E. (2015) Quantitative sex differences in response to the dissolution of a romantic relationship. *Evolutionary Behavioural Sciences*, 9(4), 270–282.

Smith, A. and Anderson, M. (2016) 5 facts about online dating. *FactTank*, Washington: Pew Research Center. www.pewresearch.org/fact-tank/2016/02/29/5-facts-about-online-dating. Accessed 25 July 2017.

Part II

Looking forward – looking back

Chapter 4

How we do relationships

Working out what went wrong in the past, and ways to avoid the same mistakes, is a powerful motivator. This chapter consequently looks at how we 'do' adult relationships and what influences our ability to be close. Each individual's personality and response to stress affects the way they cope with being in a close relationship without losing their individuality. Some people feel merged, stifled or stuck the closer their relationship becomes, while for others becoming closer boosts their confidence and feelings of selfhood.

Adaptive strategies

There are many reasons relationships make us feel uncomfortable, which often reflect ways we've been treated in the past. When we feel uncomfortable, we use adaptive strategies that helped us overcome unpleasant feelings when we were young. These can begin in the early days of life, when we first begin adjusting to the environment we live in and care we receive. For instance, babies who are left to cry may learn that there's no point in bawling; it makes no difference. In families who don't show much emotion, and who have a stoical approach to distress, these babies may go on to learn that needs aren't welcomed. As adults, they may become self-contained and unemotional, disliking neediness and offering poor support in a crisis. On the other hand, babies who are *sometimes* left to cry, and *sometimes* picked up, learn a different lesson. For them, there's every reason to scream louder, as sometimes this achieves the attention they crave. It's understandable that they then 'cry louder' as adults too, by exaggerating their distress, threatening to leave and lashing out.

Being exposed to the same caregiver(s) for many years, and unconsciously using the same behaviours in our relationships with them, we may continue to use them in our closest adult relationship(s). Usually, partners, parents and caregivers all do the very best they can, given the circumstances, and would be horrified to think they could have caused distress to someone they love. Nonetheless, we all end up with some feeling of deficit, however small, and fall in love expecting that the relationship will fix this.

Internal Working Model

On the basis of experience, we develop what psychologist John Bowlby (1973) called an 'Internal Working Model', a representation of the world we inhabit. This model tells us what to expect of the world and others, organising our behaviour and the meaning we make of our partner's behaviour too. Furthermore, we all have internal scripts that contain rules for conduct in different situations and under different circumstances. Rarely do we stop to think of alternatives to the meaning we make; we just assume we know, based on experience. However, we may find ourselves attempting to either avoid or replicate some of the behaviours, scripts and ways of thinking that we've acquired. This may be conscious or just another unconscious adaptation that we'd never notice unless pushed to think about it.

We approach adult romantic relationships full of hope that this time we'll be treated in ways we long for. Unfortunately, we're perversely drawn to people who, on the surface, appear to be just what we need but who turn out to reproduce the relationship dynamics we actually need to avoid. It's astonishing that we're able to find partners who fit our need to conquer early life relationship distress so well. Often, partners do meet those needs, at least for a while, and provide the space for personal development and emotional repair. Sometimes, though, we outgrow the relationship and need to move on to a different one with other challenges. Sometimes, too, we may both do all the growing we need and settle for each other permanently, negotiating life's ups and downs together.

Disappointment

Ideally, then, relationships *should* allow us to grow and flourish but, sometimes, we just end up feeling disappointed that our partner wasn't the person we hoped they'd be. Couples who feel comfortably separate and reasonably confident may be able to rethink and renegotiate their relationship in ways that do end up conquering the personal emotional challenges they face. However, many couples find themselves in relationships where there is, instead, a perpetual stalemate with no growth possible.

A contributory factor can be not just dashed hopes, but each partner's expectation of – or 'transference' towards – the other. If we've grown to expect poor treatment, it's understandable that we may misread our partner's intentions and be hurt or take offence when none was intended. Furthermore, underlying fear of becoming too close leads many couples to sabotage their own relationships, frequently by constantly arguing. You may yearn for intimacy and even blame your partner for not being closer, but if deep down you worry that you may be hurt if you become too close, or that your partner will like you less if they know you better, relationship conflict will avoid this risk. However, as well as having a poor effect on health, chronic conflict reduces quality of life, performance and can damage the whole family, so there are good reasons not to fight.

Parents' relationship

The way we related in our original families is imprinted on the brain and affects the way we relate to others as adults, particularly our partners. As well as bringing a set of our own expectations to the relationship, we also bring a model of the way our parents were together, which may influence our own behaviour and attitudes. For instance, witnessing our parents' battles can make us believe terrible rows are normal, so that we don't appreciate the damage anger and fighting may do. Partners who don't come from a similar background may find rows terrifying and completely withdraw, giving the impression of rejection. Their parents' battles are so awful for some people that they can't bear any conflict at all and are unable to engage with the mildest disagreements.

Some parents hide their differences so that their children never see how these were resolved and grow up with no ability to manage quarrels. They may fear any kind of disagreement because they can't imagine how it will end. It's made worse if parents split but there was no hint of a problem beforehand. This can make it seem as though a single argument could end a relationship. Fears about this may make it difficult for someone to express their needs and can lead to withdrawal, resentment and depression.

Family messages

It isn't just how our parents dealt with conflict that can influence us as adults. Without being aware of it, we absorb messages from our families and wider social groups that influence our thinking, behaviour and what we find acceptable in our relationships. Accordingly, a massive problem for many relationships is simply that partners misunderstand each other, misreading one another's style and culture.

As well as relating to wider societal, global, community and religious contexts, families have their own micro-cultures which may be unfamiliar to the other partner, even though on the surface their backgrounds may appear very similar. For instance, many of us assume there is a right and wrong way to 'do' family celebrations and can be hugely upset by quite subtle differences, such as whether to open Christmas stockings before or after breakfast, or when and what to eat for the Christmas meal. It can be interesting to consider what different family members' rules or mottos would be around issues such as religion, money, race, emotion, sex, food, appearance, celebrations, education, secrecy, sharing, work, gender, politics, alcohol, health or technology.

Scripts

The way each partner thinks and the meaning they make needs to be openly discussed. Otherwise, misattributions are likely, whereby couples completely mistake what they each mean and intend. Few of us realise that we are constantly responding to 'scripts' developed as we grew up that determine how to behave, think and feel. We're often completely unaware of the rules we've created, and which govern us, yet we're quick to notice when a partner fails to comply. Unless these rules are made explicit, the other partner may be baffled, remain in ignorance or just believe something that was never meant.

Try the exercise below to see if you can identify some of the areas you may need to discuss. For instance, few couples talk about what would constitute an affair or unacceptable relationship, as most assume they share the same beliefs. However, you and your partner may have very different ideas about whether it's OK to have coffee with an old flame, text a work colleague or hug your neighbour. What would you find completely intolerable and what can be negotiated?

Exercise: Topics for discussion

Fidelity

- Discuss behaviours that are unacceptable to you and might constitute infidelity, such as texting, sexting, sharing partially clothed or nude photographs, flirting, going for drinks, kissing, intimate touch, oral sex, intercourse.

Your ex-partners

- How much contact with your ex is acceptable?
- Are you comfortable meeting your partner's ex or having them meet yours?
- Is it OK to be friends with your ex?
- Can your ex come to your home?
- Do you send greetings cards to your ex?
- What would be overstepping the mark?
- How much is it appropriate to tell about your previous relationship(s)?

Your families

- How much contact will you have with your families?
- Will you both attend family events?
- How much financial support will you be offering your families?
- Are you considering changing your will?
- How would you feel if a member of your partner's family – such as an elderly parent or a child – wanted to live with you?
- Is it understood that you'll always be available if your family need you or are there limits on your availability?

Events

- What are your expectations for celebrations?
- Do you like expensive presents or do you prefer token gifts?
- On your birthday, would you prefer a romantic evening for two, a family celebration or to share the occasion with friends?
- How do you feel about surprises?

Holidays

- How do you like to spend holidays?
- Do you prefer to be just the two of you or do you like to travel with a crowd?
- Would you mind if your partner wanted a holiday without you?
- Who'll be responsible for booking holidays?
- How will you pay for holidays?

Hobbies

- How much time and money is it OK to spend on hobbies?
- Do you like to be involved in your partner's hobbies?
- Or for them to be involved with your interests?

Space

- How much time do you like to spend alone?
- Are there particular times when you need space?
- How would you know if your partner was feeling a bit stifled or neglected?

Drink and drugs

- How much alcohol is it OK to drink?
- Is it all right to drink during the day?
- Is recreational drug use part of your life?
- What would be unacceptable?

Household

- What do you expect of each other in terms of housework and DIY?
- How will you decide on decorations, furniture, etc.?
- Which of you is more keen on gardening?

Technology

- How much time is OK to spend playing computer games?
- Will your partner have access to your passwords?
- Can you use your phone, tablet or laptop while you're watching TV together, in bed or during meals?
- Do you prefer to eat at the table or in front of the TV?

Money

- Are you comfortable sharing your money?
- Would you like a joint bank account?
- Do you think you should each have responsibility for your own money and savings?
- If you go out, who should pay?

Finances

Partners often have differing approaches to finances, and can find themselves with unsatisfactory arrangements, simply because one partner took them for granted. Consequently, willingness to be accommodating can lead to resentment if it feels as though too much has been assumed or expected. The way money was managed in your previous relationship may influence what you want or expect in this one. You may have strong feelings about this if you feel you were financially disadvantaged last time. Or if you were responsible for managing the bills, you might assume it will be expected this time too – perhaps to the surprise of your new partner. If you don't make assumptions, and aren't squeamish about clarifying what you want, you'll both know where you stand.

Even if the way you and your partner handled money suited you in your last relationship, you may feel differently now. For instance, many older homeowners choose not to sell up and pool resources so they can keep their house as a legacy for their children. Others value the freedom that selling up offers. If your family is surprised by your decisions – about finances or any other issues – their views can be unsettling and make you question arrangements that felt comfortable. It's therefore important for you to agree what works for the two of you and try to avoid doing what one or both of you think you ought to do even when it doesn't work.

Needs

If you find it difficult to communicate about everyday arrangements, it may be even harder to discuss emotional matters. Many of us are reluctant to admit we have needs, or we expect our partners to know better than we do what these are. We then look for ways to influence and position partners to help us meet our needs and avoid our fears, without asking for what we want or acknowledging what we're doing, even to ourselves. Some hidden fears have a powerful influence on relationship dynamics. Many couples unconsciously collude to maintain a way of being together, which often satisfies neither but prevents change. For some couples, becoming closer is a risk, creating the danger of being hurt, abandoned or of having inadequacies revealed.

It's easier said than done to identify hidden fears and vulnerabilities, let alone to change them. If you're now single or in a new relationship, presumably you *have* experienced change. However, it's easy to slide back into the same old patterns. Though perhaps you wanted your previous relationship to be different, you may both have found it safer to stick with what you knew, even if that meant a permanent stalemate. The quiz below may help you to spot some of your buried concerns and to notice whether you're repeating mistakes in your new relationship. If so, you may want to consider how much difference would be tolerable for each of you and what lies beneath your need to continue as you are or were.

Quiz: Buried concerns

1. Your partner had a bad day at work and starts to cry. Do you:
   a) Give them some space.
   b) Tell them to get a grip.
   c) Give them a hug.
   d) Tell them you empathise – you've also had a bad day.
2. You're making dinner and your partner tries to cuddle you. Do you:
   a) Tell them this isn't an appropriate time – maybe later.
   b) Push them away.
   c) Cuddle them back.
   d) Cuddle them back and try to take things further.
3. You text your partner a loving message in the middle of the day and they don't reply. Do you:
   a) Feel hurt but do nothing.
   b) Not expect a reply.
   c) Assume they're busy.
   d) Send several more texts and call if they don't respond.
4. On Valentine's Day your partner gives you a card with a message that they're treating you to dinner at your favourite restaurant that night. However, you've been dropping hints about a jacket you like. Do you:

    a) Feel disappointed and hurt that your partner hadn't listened, but say nothing.
    b) You're not bothered; you'll buy the jacket yourself.
    c) Love the gesture and look forward to a romantic evening.
    d) Refuse to go to the dinner unless your partner gets you the jacket.

5. Your new partner turns up to visit your family with a huge bunch of flowers – your mother has terrible hay fever. Do you:
    a) Say nothing; the flowers are a lovely thought.
    b) Buy an expensive bottle of wine instead.
    c) Tell your family about the flowers but leave them in the car for now.
    d) Berate your partner for being so thoughtless.

6. Your date wants to get another bottle of wine – you've had enough to drink. Do you:
    a) Agree and drink with them.
    b) Let them order the bottle and then order a coffee for yourself.
    c) Say they're welcome to another glass but you'll just have a coffee.
    d) Lecture them on their drinking habits.

7. There's a spider in the bath and your partner is clearly terrified. Do you:
    a) Run away – you don't like spiders either.
    b) Laugh at them, but remove the spider.
    c) Remove the spider and check there are no more.
    d) Tell them not to be so pathetic.

8. There's a spider in the bath and you're terrified. Your partner is in the bedroom next door. Do you:
    a) Leave the bathroom as quickly as you can.
    b) Run the tap and flush the spider away.
    c) Ask your partner to help you remove the spider.
    d) Scream.

9. You're absolutely shattered and just want an early night, but your partner wants to make love. Do you:
    a) Make love; you don't want to upset your partner.
    b) Say you're too tired and sleep in the spare room to be on the safe side.
    c) Say you're tired but a quick non-sexual cuddle would be nice.

    d)   Cry – you can't believe they're being so selfish when you're tired.

10. You're given tickets for a concert you know your partner will hate. Do you:

    a)   Give the tickets away.

    b)   Not mention the concert but go by yourself or with a friend who likes the music.

    c)   Arrange to go with a friend and tell your partner how excited you are.

    d)   Make your partner go with you – they need to appreciate your musical taste.

Mostly As

You worry about getting things wrong, try not to inconvenience anyone and rarely ask for help, but you risk both becoming resentful and annoying others because you're so reluctant to say what you want. You probably feel showing needs is dangerous, and your underlying fear may be rejection.

Mostly Bs

You like to be independent and you aren't keen on fuss or emotion. You probably come from a self-contained family where everyone 'just got on with it'. You're good at taking care of yourself and dislike neediness in yourself or others. You rarely express needs but, when you do want something, you probably *tell* what you want rather than *ask*. Your underlying fear may be of vulnerability.

Mostly Cs

You're quite good at taking care of yourself and don't feel threatened by other people's needs. You're usually able to ask for what you want and to confront issues that worry you. Consequently, you may be more aware of underlying fears.

Mostly Ds

You probably become disappointed when what you imagine doesn't happen in real life. You may feel your partner should know what you're thinking and be upset when they don't. You might like your relationship with your partner to be closer, but your underlying fear may be of intimacy.

Partner as everything

The idea of 'companionate marriage', in which a couple are friends and see the relationship as a partnership rather than an arrangement, is relatively recent and not that widespread around the world – yet many of us wholeheartedly believe this is the right or only way to be. However, the idea that one person can fulfil all the needs of another is unreasonable and creates far too much pressure on relationships. You may, for instance, enjoy a completely different day out with a sibling or friend than you would with your partner. Similarly, you may have many shared interests or none at all. Some people expect to spend most of their time with their partner, but find they become moody if they don't have time alone or with friends and family. In other words, different people and situations fulfil different needs in our lives and we shouldn't expect one person to be able to provide everything we want.

Couples who are openly appreciative of each other, respectful of each other's feelings and available to one another's needs are more likely to feel comfortable being separate too. They each trust the other will keep them in mind and don't fear that being close will mean losing their identity, nor that being apart sometimes will damage their relationship. Such couples are more likely to risk sharing their feelings and don't necessarily feel offended or damaged when they disagree. Others, however, feel anxious if they're too different from their partner. This can lead to attempts to curb the partner's activities and considerable distress – which may be expressed as anger – when they're absent or have different ideas.

As a young baby, we each learn that our mother is a separate person. Then, as we grow up, we must learn to feel comfortable on our own *and* in intimate connection with others. This is known as 'differentiation', and there is much research to suggest that effective differentiation contributes to successful couple relationships. Fear of becoming lost in a relationship, so that individuality and sense of self is sacrificed, can make people either avoid intimate connection or, alternatively, become too clingy if they feel their partner is necessary to make them feel whole. The slightest sense of separation can cause huge stress and lead to irrational demands and fury, which the person probably can't fully understand themselves.

Personal change

It's quite extraordinary that so many of us manage to find a partner who has experienced similar life events to ourselves, especially when it comes to separation and loss. The developmental potential offered by relationships means that we enter them full of hope that they'll provide an opportunity to put right some of the issues from the past. Many couples learn a great deal from each other and find they experience soothing and emotional growth. However, the more difficult your previous experience was, the harder it may be to use another relationship effectively, giving and taking whatever's necessary to feel safe. Instead, the relationship may provide the latest experience of damage and difficulty. Some of this is affected by each partner's ability to deal with disappointment, especially finding out that your new love is not as perfect as you hoped they'd be. Perhaps your previous relationship involved long years of hanging on, trying to provoke change in your partner. However, adjustment, acceptance and mutual understanding begin with personal change – that elusive ability to differentiate.

Hoping for particular qualities in another gives away personal control and volition. If you're dependent on someone else to make you feel OK, you'll be disappointed again and again, as their hopes will probably be just as urgent and dependent on what *you* do. Once you feel comfortable with yourself, it's much easier to discuss what you need with confidence and curiosity, rather than on some level assuming you're entitled to the other's care or that you don't deserve it. Couples who feel comfortable with themselves are far more able to negotiate objectively and care for one another without an intrusive agenda. For instance, partners who genuinely feel responsible for their own wellbeing usually offer a containing, non-judgemental and caring presence, which calms the other and allows them to develop their own sense of personal responsibility.

Snooping

This ability to differentiate is more important than ever, as modern relationships are subject to new and growing stresses now that technology plays such a big part in our lives. In the past, suspicious partners might go through the other's pockets, peek at their diary or lurk around trying to overhear their telephone calls. Now that we have mobile phones, e-mail and instant messaging, there's so much more to have a snoop at. As it's possible to have a conversation without speaking out loud, and to share film and photos instantly without your partner knowing, technology has provided both increased temptation to have another relationship, and the means to do so sneakily. This gives partners much more to doubt, making modern relationships potentially a lot less trusting. And it isn't just fear of affairs that makes people pry; sometimes they do it just to try to find out what their partner is thinking.

When there is secrecy, the other partner may be tempted to start snooping even when they'd normally respect privacy and feel this is wrong, possibly because they feel hurt and excluded. Sometimes, it isn't so much that someone is secretive as that they don't bother to share information until the last minute, disliking being questioned and so refusing to tell or changing details without saying so. Not only can this be frustrating and irritating but it can convey a casual approach to the other's partner's needs, which may be construed as uncaring or disrespectful.

Clearly, reading your partner's texts or e-mails without their permission shouldn't happen but, once snooping starts, it tends to grow in frequency and intensity. It makes sense, then, for you to discuss early in a new relationship how you communicate and how much sharing you feel comfortable with. It's much harder to be sneaky once someone has explicitly stated they don't expect you to look at their mail, phone, computer or tablet without their permission. Some people feel entitled to check up on their partners and even use surveillance equipment or hack into their online accounts. This is never acceptable, however anxious you may be or your partner may say they are. It's another reason for negotiating disclosure in advance and finding ways to calm yourself if being unable to get at all your partner's information unsettles you.

Those who don't like being questioned, and resent giving any information at all, often come from fairly closed families whose members tend to look after themselves, rather than each other, and where feelings are rarely discussed or displayed. In fact, somewhere along the line they might even have developed the idea that their thoughts, needs and feelings were harmful or that it was shaming to have them. This is particularly the case in families where children's clamour for attention is dismissed. It's often because parents are tired or busy, but also sometimes because needs are seen as distasteful.

Some families show emotion all the time, which is great so long as the emotion is appropriate to the situation and not exaggerated or understated, or if only one or some family members are allowed to be 'emotional'. This doesn't help children learn to manage their feelings, especially when it means parents are inconsistent or unpredictable. This makes children closely monitor their families and guess their moods so that they won't get into trouble. As adults, they can then become very upset if their partner isn't communicating, as the case of Vin and Ollie demonstrates.

Vin and Ollie

Vin comes from a tactile and emotionally expressive family. They could be arguing vehemently one minute and then forget all about it the next. Both his parents hugged and kissed him and each other a great deal, and they were always telling Vin they loved him. Vin's mother was very sensitive and often told Vin he could always confide in her. However, her sensitivity meant she could become upset and cry over the slightest thing, often turning to Vin's sister for comfort or to complain about the way Vin or his dad had treated her. Sometimes when she was upset, Vin's mum would smack or punch him. The more upset *she* was, the more other family members always seemed to become angry with him. Vin rarely knew what he'd done wrong, just that it was hard to get things right and that something about him upset people. Sometimes his dad became involved, and yelled at him for upsetting his mum, but it still wasn't clear what he should do to change.

The unpredictable and often scary world Vin occupied was best managed by keeping to himself and looking after his own needs. Trying to work out what other people wanted was too difficult. This could infuriate his mum, who would question him about what he was thinking, telling him he was clearly upset and upsetting her by failing to tell her what was wrong. Usually, Vin didn't feel upset and couldn't think of anything to tell his mother. If he did need to talk to her, though, she'd often be angry, saying, 'What *now*, Vin?!', as though he never stopped bothering her.

Ollie came from a much more buttoned-up family. His parents were rarely emotionally expressive but made sure Ollie and his two brothers were well cared for. They were seldom angry but often expressed disappointment if he or his brothers didn't do what was expected. On these occasions, they'd sometimes say they were too sad to speak to him, completely withdrawing for hours or days at a time. Ollie's brothers also learned to withdraw when displeased, so there was a great deal of what he called 'moodiness' in Ollie's world. If they were pleased with the children, however, Ollie's parents would always say so, often comparing Ollie and his brothers so that their relationships became quite competitive.

Even as a tiny tot, Ollie would often 'muck around'. Playing the fool and doing tricks made the family laugh, though there were times when it just got him into trouble. This was better than being ignored though, and Ollie would try anything to get his parents' attention, especially on days when they weren't speaking to someone.

Vin and Ollie's relationship was characterised by Ollie's attempts to get Vin's attention in any way he could. He was frightened when Vin was quiet and withdrawn and badgered him continuously to talk to him, which only made Vin withdraw more. Ollie was so desperate to get Vin's attention that he started flaunting other relationships, cutting himself and disappearing for days at a time. Ollie didn't consciously realise that his behaviour was attention-seeking; to him it just seemed to be evidence of his suffering. He thought it was clear to everyone that Vin was treating him badly. Occasionally, Vin would completely blow his top and, after a huge row, there would be a brief period of calm.

Eventually, they both realised this was unbearable. Vin said he'd leave unless Ollie got some help. Ollie agreed to consider therapy if Vin would too. To their surprise, therapy *was* helpful, as they began to recognise how their relationship reflected their underlying fears and feelings of helplessness. They're not sure whether they can still be partners, though they both think they'll always be friends.

An additional problem for insecure couples like Vin and Ollie is that they tend not to notice the positive aspects of their relationship. Instead, they're highly attuned to anything negative and even to misperceive behaviours that are intended to be positive. Indeed, couples like this are even poor at recognising positive facial expressions, making arguments more likely and reconciliation much harder (Niedenthal et al., 2002). Such conflict is the focus of Chapter 5, exploring how the way we do relationships can lead to so much distress.

Remember: If you change, your partner will respond differently too.

Bibliography

Bowlby, J. (1973) *Attachment and Loss: Volume 2. Separation, Anxiety and Anger*, New York: Basic Books.

Niedenthal, P. M., Brauner, M., Robin, L. and Innes-Ker, A. H. (2002) Adult attachment and the perception of facial expression of emotion. *Journal of Personality and Social Psychology*, 82(3), 419–433.

Titelman, P. (2014) *Differentiation of Self*, Hove: Routledge.

Chapter 5

Why couples argue

It's hard to believe, but some of the most miserable and volatile relationships are the most stable. Painful it may be, but many couples are locked into battles with their partners that, however hard they try, they can't seem to change even by leaving. Indeed, they may not want to leave until they've conquered whatever's wrong with the relationship. If they attempt counselling, they usually claim to have tried 'everything'. What they may actually have done is to continually repeat a pernicious pattern from which they can't escape. Maybe the row is constantly simmering. There may be endless bickering or periods of calm followed by huge eruptions. Commonly, neither partner is aware of the triggers or even able to remember what each argument was about.

Moments of confusion and vulnerability provoke rows like this, making them feel particularly crucial and deadly. But the row doesn't get anywhere. The same doors are slammed, the same threats are made. Afterwards, there is the same anxious and sick feeling of failure and rejection.

A fight for existence

This may be something you recognise well and/or what you're desperate to avoid in your next relationship. For some people, arguments are more than just a way to resolve everyday tensions and disagreements. Though they may occur on a daily basis, these are not ordinary quarrels – they're a fight for existence. Whether they're constant or occasional eruptions, thoroughly damaging rows are often triggered instantly, a knee-jerk flight to fury that seems unavoidable. If they're really severe, you may feel stuck in a continuous cycle of negativity and escalation that leaves you traumatised. As a result, you and your partner will both strengthen your defences, so that a lifelong power struggle ensues. Though both of you may long to be understood, to feel heard or for the arguing to stop, neither of you may feel able to do anything differently, to acknowledge the other's hurt or maybe even to recognise how much this is hurting you. Indeed, the psychiatrist and relationships researcher Henry Dicks (1967) said that couples have only one fight, but they have it over and over again.

You're not necessarily off the hook if you don't argue. There are other behaviours that can be just as unbearable to experience or witness – long silences or sulks and refusal to talk can go on for months, with no doubt that the weaponry of *this* war is withdrawal, and it can be just as damaging. Even though the arguing – or sulking or silences – is so harrowing and disruptive, it seems impossible to prevent. When the fight feels so real and present, it's hard to believe that what makes it so painful now may have happened long ago. Couples are often unconsciously drawn to each other to put right long-buried emotional injuries that remain unresolved. We enter relationships full of hope, expecting them to make life better, and the disappointment when they don't may feel unbearable.

Honeymoon blindness

Sometimes, even when you hated the fights in a previous relationship, you find yourself in an identical battle in a new relationship which originally felt full of promise. The trouble is that you don't necessarily see the inevitable faults and flaws that become abundantly clear later on. As we learned in Chapter 1, hormones associated with pair bonding blind us to aspects of the relationship we dislike and enhance those qualities that we want to see. We may even see what isn't there at all. In particular, the hormone oxytocin increases feelings of bonding and distracts partners from each other's drawbacks.

Somehow, we can be unconsciously attracted to someone who will challenge us in familiar ways. So if you had, say, very critical parents, you could find yourself attracted to a critical partner too. Because the exciting circumstances, your hopes and oxytocin conceal this initially, such a partner may seem very laid back and *un*critical in the early days of the relationship. This can make it appear that they've become critical over time, but it's more likely to be your perception that's changed, with your partner noticing that *you* aren't as perfect as they thought either.

The habitual dynamic that is then created between you and your partner is partly down to how you treat each other and partly about how you expect to be treated.

- If you're confident in yourself, and don't feel too inhibited about stating your needs and negotiating, you may find a way of collaborating to manage and minimise the irritating aspects of the relationship.
- If you're too confident, you won't be able to recognise your own part in the relationship's problems and may take responsibility only for making a poor relationship choice. This leaves you with no way of influencing what happens, because all the onus is on your partner to change.
- If, on the other hand, your confidence is low, and you're used to being treated as though you're not good enough, you'll probably feel blamed and take on the responsibility for whatever's wrong in the relationship, even though you may mightily resent this. You may even regard your partner with suspicion and respond as though you're being put down even when this isn't happening. This may be irritating enough to make your partner actually react as though you're being a nuisance and to genuinely comment negatively on your behaviour, as happened to Carol.

Carol

Carol was an only child brought up by her mother in a single-parent family. They felt very close and it mattered to Carol that her mother supported and approved of her life choices and behaviour – but her mother constantly found fault. Whenever Carol didn't do exactly what her mother wanted, she told Carol she wasn't behaving like a loving daughter. Her mother probably didn't realise how hurtful she was to Carol. She may even have thought she was helping her.

Once she started having relationships, Carol found herself behaving like her mother. She'd exaggerate and tell partners they weren't good enough or loving enough if they didn't do what she wanted, which she experienced as rejection. They, in turn, accused her of being selfish and neurotic. In all her relationships, and without realising, Carol found herself trying to get one over on partners, treating them as though they were out to get her, even when their behaviour was kind and thoughtful. Supportive relationships were rare, however, as Carol seemed drawn to partners who were critical and demanding.

It wasn't until after a particularly painful argument and threatened breakup that one of them, Chris, insisted they seek couple counselling. At this point, the motivation wasn't to repair their relationship but to help them both work out why they were repeating the same painful patterns time and time again. This wasn't easy. In counselling, they both vied for the counsellor's approval and attention, again fighting for recognition and acceptance. Eventually, Carol started to recognise that her knee-jerk response to any comment relating to her, even when it was positive, was to defend herself. At last, she realised that her treatment of Chris was often unkind. Chris also acknowledged his part, realising that he was a perfectionist who took it personally if all aspects of his life weren't entirely problem-free. Appreciating that this was impossible, especially in relationships, was difficult, but they found they could help one another with this and that it became much easier over time.

The important point about what happened to Carol was that she provoked critical behaviour, chose partners who were critical and was highly critical herself when she felt threatened. Somewhere deep inside she was looking for the opportunity to overcome her not-good-enough feelings by defending herself successfully, something she hadn't been able to do with her mother. It would have been better for her if she'd been attracted to kinder, more balanced people. However, the apparently confident partners she chose also felt they were not good enough, but had learned to cope with this by squashing that feeling and, instead, creating a belief that they were better than others. People who manage to completely avoid their negative feelings in this way will often wholeheartedly respond to lack of self-esteem by adding to it, being critical and disparaging the other's efforts and feelings. Awful and unacceptable though the experience was, it was this treatment that Carol recognised and which gave her the challenge she sought to prove her worth.

This happens a lot, because it takes someone who is secure within themselves to respond to others with genuine concern and to accept care without demands or suspicion. If one of a couple *does* feel 'good enough', they can provide the positivity and care to help their less secure partner to feel more confident too. But if both of a couple are deeply insecure – even when they appear self-assured on the surface – their lack of self-worth is liable to escalate. This is how people who are apparently different can end up in a similar dynamic as they did in previous relationships.

Proving worth

People often manage feelings of insecurity either by desperately trying to prove their value or by overriding and dismissing their feelings to the extent that they deny having them at all. Some people seem to have great confidence and to sail through life without problems. This is very appealing to someone with low self-esteem who may feel flattered that anyone so self-assured is interested in them. Similarly, those who are too confident may find it satisfying to be with someone low in self-worth. They may feel they're helping them or enjoy criticising their 'faults'. The faults they pick may reflect aspects of themselves that they don't like or want. Seeing them in their partner may, therefore, be very uncomfortable or they may, in some way, enjoy attacking them.

Understandably, couples like this are often drawn to each other. The 'low-esteem', criticised partner uses the opportunity to see whether the critical, confident one will finally recognise their worth. Needless to say, this is highly unlikely. Often, the apparently confident one isn't really very confident at all, a sign of which is their readiness to be critical.

Suppressed negative feelings don't go away. Dissociation from the pain of not-good-enough feelings may mean they're replaced by a show of confidence or even arrogance and grandiosity. Then, when a partner's lack of self-esteem reminds someone of their own insecurity, their instant reaction may be to criticise. Meanwhile, the apparently insecure partner will probably respond with a powerful defence of their worth, arguing the case that they really are good enough, desperate for their 'confident' partner to agree. There's little chance that they will, however. Often unconsciously, some critical partners actually set up situations guaranteed to make the other show their neediness and protest their value, which temporarily relieves their own insecurity.

Sharon and Gavin

Even though Sharon knew Gavin liked to have downtime when he came home from work, she'd pounce on him as soon as he came through the door and ask him to do some job or want his opinion about something. Though this made him grumpy, and he asked her not to do it, she justified it by insisting that seeking his opinion or help showed respect. She also thought this might avoid his criticism, because he would *always* complain if he wasn't consulted. However, her timing made it much more likely that Gavin would criticise because he was tired and distracted.

It would have been noticeable to an outsider that Sharon always took the initiative about planning anything, from when to do the housework to holidays and investments. Sharon thought this showed her willingness and energy, but Gavin just said she was being controlling. This did, however, let Gavin off the hook if anything went wrong, something he was secretly afraid of.

Letting Gavin take responsibility for a change may have demonstrated the difficulties of some of the tasks that Sharon complained about or asked for help with. This would also have helped to share her burden of responsibility. It would have been interesting to see how they both managed genuine collaboration rather than the damaging perpetrator-victim dynamic they'd fallen into, playing both roles magnificently.

No objectivity

Both of a couple can, like Sharon and Gavin, each genuinely believe they're the one doing the best for the relationship and that they're the victim. Both being so firmly convinced of their own position, they're unable to see their situation objectively or appreciate their own part in it. Those who are used to feeling blamed may also blame themselves, but without being able to see which aspects of the issue are their responsibility. They may, for instance, see the most unacceptable aspects of their behaviour as providing an acceptable solution. Equally, they may be unable to evaluate aspects of their partner's behaviour that are abusive and need to be addressed. They come to see everything as having equal value, and can't effectively judge which of their own and their partner's complaints are relatively trivial and which are genuinely unfair or unkind. Likewise, those who so effectively separate themselves from negative feelings, and convince themselves of their superior worth and rightness, are at risk of cruel and unfeeling behaviour, of which they may be completely unaware.

Being unable to effectively or dispassionately assess what's happening in a relationship can make it very easy for partners to become like a pair of squabbling siblings, particularly if they really did have a competitive relationship with brothers and sisters. However, even only children can behave in this way, carrying on as though some unseen presence is judging which of them is right, wrong or better than the other. At this point, common sense is lost. Neither thinks about their objectives, just about protecting their own position and proving they're 'better' than the other. Winning – whatever that means – becomes terrifically important and may lead people to unwittingly behave in ways that aren't in their own longer-term interests.

There's often a great deal of unfinished business like this from our pasts, causing hurt that can be confused with current feelings about our relationship. That feelings from the past can be so easily evoked by current events helps to explain why relatively trivial matters can assume such great significance. It can then be difficult to stop unhelpful behaviours, like Carol's or Sharon and Gavin's.

Feeling heard

Once a row has begun, it can be difficult to end. Often, feeling heard is a major motivator for continuing an argument. This can also connect with frustrated feelings from early in our lives. As we learned in Chapter 4, as a crying baby, you needed to make yourself heard to attract attention and have your discomfort fixed. At the time, your instincts told you that this was a desperate matter of survival. At later times in your life when you don't feel heard, or feel vulnerable, the same feeling may come up and make you feel just as desperate. This isn't even necessarily triggered by anything particularly important. It can be random or inappropriate, such as when you're arguing about the direction teaspoons face in the dishwasher. You may feel that you can't let this go, and even follow your partner around carrying on about it all.

More stable partners are baffled by the sort of desperate behaviour that can surface in a row and do manage to be placatory or to remove themselves until things have calmed down. For others, pointing out that the loading of cutlery is not, in fact, life-threatening, may provoke a furious response: 'It's not about that!' And it isn't. It's about not feeling good enough and not really knowing what you've done wrong. If its origins lie in your experience of being a tiny baby and crying to be noticed, it makes sense that you'd cry louder and more heartily if your carer didn't always come. As a baby, the feeling of urgency *would* have been appropriate but, as an adult, there's no need to behave as though it's a life or death matter when your partner doesn't hear you or see your point of view.

Babies who learn there's no point in crying as it won't make any difference repress their distress and detach from their feelings. As adults, they can make matters worse when the other partner is upset by belittling, ignoring or rejecting any feelings the partner expresses, just as they've learned to do with their own emotions.

Some people learn to take care of their carers at a very young age. It may be that their mothers or carers became upset or angry when they cried or that, as they grew older, they were expected to take emotional care of their mums. As adults, they'll often take criticisms to heart, finding it really important to get relationships right. For instance, even when their partner is being unreasonable or uncaring, they may believe this could change if only they themselves tried harder to please. Or they may leave, believing this is what's wanted – only to be met with more criticism, because the partner who told them to go now feels abandoned. Either way, partners who exaggerate and cry for attention often amaze the other the day after a row when they behave as though nothing happened. Because they exaggerate, they expect others to do the same. Consequently, they won't take seriously any mild-mannered requests or protests, and are unlikely to accept that their partner wasn't abandoning them when they left – even when they told them to go!

Paddy and Dilip

Paddy was brought up in a home where his father's needs were prioritised. The children had to creep around so as not to disturb their dad when he was working, sleeping, reading the newspaper or trying to watch TV. He could become very angry if he felt the children were being too noisy or needy, and this often made their mother cry. Paddy and his siblings would take care of their mum at these times. They thought of her as highly strung and did their best not to upset her.

As he grew up, Paddy tried to avoid conflict and to take care of people, as this was something he felt good at. In his mind, his solicitous care of Dilip meant that Dilip shouldn't be angry with him or make demands, and he couldn't understand why they seemed to argue so much or so fiercely. Dilip, on the other hand, came from a family where everyone spoke their mind. There were frequent rows, with different family members banding together to take sides. His parents often changed their minds about how they wanted the children and each other to behave, so Dilip learned to second-guess people and not to trust what they said.

Dilip could be very angry when Paddy tried to do things for him. He would shout at him for touching his belongings or tell Paddy he was treating him as though he was stupid. Paddy would apologise and explain that he'd only been tidying up or trying to help, but Dilip would have none of this. Paddy would try to get away when this happened, so as not to antagonise Dilip further, but it would just make matters worse. Dilip would shout at Paddy and follow him, telling him that he was disrespectful and wasn't listening. Meanwhile, Paddy would protest that Dilip wasn't listening to *him*, but this seemed to make Dilip madder. Sometimes he would walk out or tell Paddy to leave. When Dilip left, he would be back after work the next day, behaving as though nothing had happened. If Paddy left, on the other hand, Dilip would send furious texts and phone repeatedly, telling him what a terrible person he was and how he'd abandoned Dilip.

Eventually, a friend who'd witnessed this several times suggested that Dilip get some help with his anger. Dilip hadn't thought of himself as angry at all. The idea that an outsider saw him this way shook him up enough to take stock of his behaviour. Meanwhile, Paddy was just as surprised that the friend wasn't blaming *him* for not looking after Dilip well enough, and he made up his mind that he really would leave if there was another row. Fortunately, though their relationship remained difficult, this marked the end of the awful arguing as, with considerable professional help, the couple developed new strategies to manage their feelings.

Not feeling heard or appreciated is so common as to be almost normal in relationships, and frequently crops up in disagreements over housework, parenting, relatives, sex or money. Often, it's the approach to discussing the issue that causes the problem. For instance, you may be a person who tries not to nag but then becomes resentful when your partner doesn't guess what you want. Your frustration is then blurted out angrily, a row ensues and you're accused of badgering. As this is exactly what you've been trying to avoid, it's like a red rag to a bull. Your partner is probably experiencing something similar, so there isn't much chance of being heard or appreciated while you're both feeling so defensive. Only if you can stand back and try to look objectively at what's going on can you successfully avoid repetitive arguments if you're both easily triggered.

Cavemen

Some people deliberately hide their feelings and then wonder why they aren't understood. Part of the problem for some men, in particular, is a feeling that it's weak to be dependent and especially to show any sort of need, so they go out of their way to show indifference. Even though their partner may be longing for – if not actually demanding – more evidence of a connection, the man behaves as though, and believes, the partner will think less of him if he shows signs of dependence or need. If he experiences any sort of threat to the relationship, he remains unable to show distress. Instead, he reacts with anger and asserts his rights over the partner and his entitlement to them, complaining of threats to his pride and property rather than a hurting heart.

Some partners rather enjoy this machismo as it saves them from having to engage emotionally. They may complain about lack of emotional intelligence, but it lets *them* control the emotional pace. It's a collusion that allows the 'blokey' partner to overtly evade emotional action and pass responsibility for feelings to the other partner. The other can then side-step emotionality if they wish, claiming it as too much for the man rather than themselves. Alternatively, they may make a big show of emotion and acting out which shames the partner and positions themselves as 'best' at feelings. This enables them to be more and more emotional as they berate the man for his lack of sensitivity.

Of course, it isn't just men who have difficulty showing feelings. Anyone can find this hard, and a lot depends on how you showed your feelings in your family of origin. How this happened is what probably feels normal and natural to you, especially if there were very open ideas about what was acceptable, either within the family as a whole or for either gender. It's common to be so acclimatised to the rules and behaviours of your own family that these continue into adulthood. As a result, partners are often treated as though they're responding to the same set of rules as yourself, whereas they may actually conform to very different rituals and expectations.

Family culture

We tend to think of culture as referring to certain religious or community ideas and practices, but every family has a culture of its own.
Consider what happens when you go to stay at someone else's house.
You don't know the drill – so do you flush the loo at night or not?
Will your host think you're rude if you don't join them in the kitchen
while they cook or do they prefer you to keep out of the way? How
can you tell if you've outstayed your welcome? What are the expectations regarding gifts? How easy do you find it to bring up such matters? Do you prefer not to discuss them but try to work them out?

You and your partner may have different ways of going about
things, and even this can lead to tension. Most of us assume that the
way we perform family rules and rituals is *the* way. In fact, we don't
usually notice what we do, although the differences become obvious when two families collide, as Duncan and Kirsty discovered.

Duncan and Kirsty

In Kirsty's family it was normal practice at meals for the last tasty
item left – a piece of pie or cake or a roast potato – to be eaten
by the most deserving person at the dinner table. So if someone
was under the weather, celebrating an achievement or had a bad
day, they'd appoint themselves as deserving. This was indicated
and accepted by the others through the custom of the deserving
one offering the goody they wanted to the others. The other diners
would all politely decline and insist the deserving person took it.

In Duncan's family, it was the custom to fight over the last por-
tions – unless guests were present. In this case, the drill was to offer
to guests – and it was considered really impolite for the guest not to
accept, whether they wanted the food or not.

So when Kirsty's brother, who'd just passed an important exam,
offered the remaining spoonful of dessert to Duncan, no one
expected Duncan to accept the dessert and gobble it up. When
he did, this led to the couple's first major row. Luckily, they both
quickly realised how different their attitudes and expectations actually were. Ultimately, this helped them not to take each other for
granted and to question some of their assumptions.

Most of us don't have an example like Kirsty and Duncan's to
wake us up to the differences in our ways of thinking and behaving.
Usually, we just go on assuming that we know what our partner

means by a certain behaviour or comment when, actually, we probably haven't a clue. The understandings that became established in a long relationship are not necessarily transferable to new relationships, but it's all too easy to forget that. What causes arguments is often really trivial, but it creates problems because of the meaning we attach to it.

The dishwasher incident

So let's say that Kirsty asks Duncan to load the dishwasher in a certain way and he does it differently. Let's say, too, that Duncan hasn't particularly been thinking about how the dishwasher is loaded. However, he does feel the dishwasher is his domain; he loads it after dinner because Kirsty cooks. This was the way jobs were shared during his previous relationship, and both he and that partner were content with this. Consequently, this is what he expects of Kirsty too. He's cross that Kirsty is interfering. It's as if she doesn't trust him, and he wants to prove he's up to the task and can even innovate.

Kirsty, however, is furious when she realises that Duncan hasn't loaded the dishwasher in the way she required. How could he be so disrespectful? If he really loved her, she thinks, he would do as she asked. This would show her that he appreciated her and that he was being considerate – as *she* will be the one to unload the dishwasher in the morning. So it's *she*, not Duncan, who'll suffer if the crockery hasn't washed properly or, worse still, if any has cracked. In Kirsty's family of origin, and in *her* last relationship, accidents and breakages were great cause for concern and never went overlooked.

Let's say now that Kirsty complains to Duncan, and he says he can't believe she's arguing over the way the dishwasher's loaded. He's thinking now that she definitely doesn't trust or respect him; she doesn't even think he can load a dishwasher. He's upset. There've been other times when he's been in trouble and hasn't known why. In fact, he's often managed to do the wrong thing and been told how useless he was – by his parents, siblings, school teachers, friends, colleagues and previous partner. Now even Kirsty thinks he's hopeless. He panics; maybe she'll dump him. He's angry to think she could end their relationship over washing up. He shouts at her. She cries and calls him a bully. She thinks it's obvious now that he doesn't love her or consider her feelings at all. She thinks they may as well call it a day.

Misunderstanding

Kirsty and Duncan wouldn't really think or behave like this because they've learned a thing or two about meaning-making and would be able to stand back and question their assumptions before leaping to such damaging conclusions. For most of us, though, meaning is assumed and accepted without question or conversation. It's relatively easy, therefore, to get into an argument over something as slight as loading the dishwasher, particularly if there are other underlying doubts and unspoken concerns. Unfortunately, the more such issues remain unrecognised and unaddressed, the more likely it is to feel unheard, unappreciated, disrespected and unloved. Hence, a minor slight can easily trigger sensitivities and feel confusingly like a massive trauma. You may not understand this when it happens, but the need it produces may feel powerful and urgent. This may simply be experienced as a wish for understanding or be a deep longing for comfort and support. Frequently, unintelligible feelings of anger, shame, humiliation or loss accompany the event.

If you can't even explain this to yourself, you have little chance of explaining it to your partner. This can leave you both assuming you're being judged and ready to make judgements about each other. Times when you most need to explain your feelings are often when it's least easy to do so, especially if this involves vulnerability or need. Your pain, or need to get out of the painful situation, may be dominating your behaviour and stopping you from thinking about what's going on for your partner. However, the ability to look at a situation from more than one perspective is essential to avoid arguing. If you can't see things from another point of view, nothing will ever change. When rowing has become intractable, arguments often aren't ever resolved, rumbling on indefinitely from one blow-up to the next, with either an uneasy truce in between or a terrible atmosphere. The quiz below may help to give an idea of how you approach arguments and the role you could play in initiating, continuing and recovering from them.

Quiz: How you argue

1. Your view of arguing is that:
    a) Arguments are sometimes inevitable.
    b) Arguments can be a good way to clear the air.
    c) Arguments are to be avoided if possible.
    d) Arguments can't usually be justified.

2. People would say that you:
   a) Are fairly even tempered.
   b) Are quite fiery.
   c) Rarely lose your temper, but really let rip when you do.
   d) Never lose your cool.
3. Rows usually start when:
   a) You're stressed or tired.
   b) You least expect it.
   c) You've had enough.
   d) You don't have rows.
4. Which one of you is best at explaining and sharing emotions?
   a) It could be either of us.
   b) I am.
   c) I don't feel the need to talk as much as my partner does.
   d) We generally feel the same way about things.
5. Rows are usually resolved if:
   a) You calm down and talk about things.
   b) You apologise.
   c) Your partner apologises.
   d) They don't develop in the first place.
6. After an argument:
   a) You often feel you've learned something.
   b) You feel shattered and upset for days.
   c) You're able to put the row behind you.
   d) If it happened, you'd make a special effort to reconnect.

Mostly As

Though you try to avoid rows, you're prepared to state your case and can become heated about something you believe in. You're probably also prepared to listen to the other side of the argument and compromise if it's necessary – though you may hope it won't be.

Mostly Bs

You often feel misunderstood and that your efforts aren't being recognised. When rows start, you may feel panicky and experience a desperate need to be heard and to fix things now. Though rows often follow the same pattern, you continue to hope that this time will be different and you'll finally be able to prove your worth.

Mostly Cs

You probably can't be bothered with rows, and either go along with your partner for the sake of a quiet life or just do your own thing regardless. You may not see the point of talking about feelings, and may see your partner as too emotional.

Mostly Ds

You and your partner probably consider yourselves to be soulmates. You rarely disagree – if you do there's usually a point of contact to be found. However, you may each be stifling your individuality and suppressing your real feelings in order to avoid conflict.

Avoiding rows

If the quiz has made you think you could be doing more to handle conflict in your relationship, there are lots of suggestions about managing arguing throughout the book, and Chapter 9 is dedicated to solutions for ways to break negative cycles. In the meantime, you may be looking for a quick fix to use the next time matters start to escalate. Counting to ten and walking away are common strategies to deal with anger, but they aren't always effective in overriding those desperate life and death feelings you may be experiencing in the middle of a row. The best way to achieve this is to have a plan which you can put into effect *before* things get really heated and your sensible brain goes offline.

Ideally, find a time when you're both calm and receptive to a positive conversation about how to manage your rows. Suggest to your partner that next time there's an argument you plan to walk away from it to try to prevent it from escalating. It may be important to share this plan so that your partner doesn't feel even more rejected when you walk off. If you can, try to get prior agreement that they won't pursue you.

Of course, this plan may be easier said than done. When it comes to it, you may feel much more like fighting than walking away, and could quickly become overtaken by strong feelings. To try to avoid this, you need to become familiar with your feelings so that you can notice what's happening in your body when an argument starts. This way you'll recognise the signs of a dispute beginning and take avoidant action as early as possible. You may also notice negative or angry thoughts, as well as changes in your body, and realise you don't have much time before the row becomes out of hand. Once you really become furious, the area of the brain that inhibits reckless behaviour – the prefrontal cortex – isn't functioning. At this point, it's no good trying to have a sensible conversation, as you'll probably either just be lashing out or too upset. That's why walking away until you've calmed down is such an excellent idea. Remember that it's not giving in to walk away – it's about taking control.

If you feel upset by your partner walking away, maybe you need to learn to take care of yourself at such times. You could walk away yourself or suggest that your partner might want some space. Don't feel rejected while they're gone. You'll be in a far better position to think and talk rationally when you've both calmed down. Bear in mind that your vulnerabilities have been roused, and you're both probably reacting to long-ago memories as well as to the immediate issue. Keep telling yourself this and you may be better able to resist the temptation to run after your partner or to feel abandoned.

Before you have a row

If noticing yourself becoming angry or upset isn't enough to stop a row, or if you stay angry after your partner has taken themselves off, try talking yourself down.

- **Ask yourself what you're trying to achieve.** What are you aiming for? Give up for now if you're trying to defend yourself or make a point. It's likely your partner isn't listening and that you'd be better off having a quiet conversation another time. In fact, give up anyway. If hackles are rising, it's too late for a dignified conversation, so leave it until another time.
- **Consider the context.** If it's late and you're tired, if the children might overhear, if either of you has been drinking or using drugs, this is not the best time for any kind of discussion. Leave it.
- **Distract yourself.** If it's hard to walk away, and you're dying to fight back, try to think of something else to do. Watch TV, sort the washing, do some gardening, tinker with the car, walk the dog, take the children to the park, anything that takes your mind off the row. Beware of phoning someone in a fury to offload while you're angry though – this may wind you up even more.

If the world was about to end

A good way to stop yourself from lashing out is to consider whether you'd still say what you're about to say if the world was about to end and these would be the last words the other person would ever hear from you. If the answer is no, don't say them. Realise that you were about to say something you'd probably have regretted, that would almost certainly cause severe damage and that may come back to bite you. Partners remember spiteful comments which can then haunt you indefinitely. Even worse, the hurt they cause can be terminal. Lashing out chips away at the love and trust you've built until there's none left and it's too late to retrieve the situation.

Though it's easy to make suggestions, and much harder to put them into practice, most couples *are* perfectly capable of making a plan together and prompting one another to walk away when things start becoming heated. If one of you can't do this, it's even more important that the other finds a way to remove themselves safely before the situation escalates further. *It is never ever OK to do anything to prevent a partner from leaving if they choose to.* Nor is it OK to prevent them from taking any children with them if they or the children are finding your behaviour threatening, even if that isn't your intention.

The next chapter considers more about how previous experience affects the way relationships are approached and conducted, and the unconscious processes affecting them.

Remember: Nobody *deliberately* sets out to have a relationship where all they do is row. If this happens, there's likely to be much more going on for each of you than is immediately apparent. You shouldn't take it personally, but you can change the argumentative behaviour by changing your own thinking and responses.

Bibliography

Dicks, H. V. (1967) *Marital Tensions: Clinical Studies Toward a Psychoanalytic Theory of Interaction*, London: Routledge & Kegan Paul.

Chapter 6

The unconscious contract

At best, couple relationships can provide an environment in which both the two individuals and the relationship itself can flourish or, at worst, each partner can stagnate in an anti-developmental conspiracy. We've already learned that, because of their backgrounds and early experience, people come to relationships with a set of hopes and expectations that they're rarely fully aware of. These expectations form a kind of unconscious relationship contract, which leaves each partner disappointed when its terms aren't fulfilled. Inevitably, relationships are unlikely to completely meet each partner's expectations, but how this is managed determines whether the couple will be enabled or disabled by the pairing. If you felt stuck or unhappy in your previous relationship, you may want to do more than cross your fingers and hope in the next one. Making a conscious effort this time to identify expectations and try to notice any unhelpful behaviour patterns that are developing will go a long way towards establishing and maintaining the stability of any new relationship.

When we start a new relationship, we're unconsciously looking to put right previous relationship difficulties, some of which will date back to childhood and some will be more recent. We may also want to redo a relationship we enjoyed or we may just, like it or not, reproduce the relationship our parents seemed to have. Whatever it is we're seeking, many of us are disappointed. Usually, we blame our partner for not turning out to be what they promised. But *did* they promise? Though we may approach commitment with vague generic hope, very few of us actually consider what it is we need or what's even possible. We may think we knew our own and our partner's weaknesses and drawbacks, but still somehow expect we'll both be magically transformed by the acquisition of a door key or a wedding ring. Remember, Prince Charming could only recognise the love of his life by the size of her feet, yet Cinderella still thought he was a good catch!

If you're entering a second or subsequent relationship, it's arguably even more important that you give proper consideration to what you want this time, and what it's going to take to achieve this. Even when both partners are expecting the same Happy Ever After, their vision of how it's enacted may be different. Psychotherapist Hugh Jenkins (2006) speaks of an invisible – and often unconscious – contract between partners directed towards the fulfilment of unmet needs. Shared conscious expectations may include elements such as companionship, sex and emotional support, but how these are experienced in practice may not be what each partner imagined. Moreover, underlying their expectations may be deeper desires, such as hoping to learn from the partner, that the partner will manage difficult emotions or take care of unliked personal traits. These odd-sounding wishes address developmental tasks that, for some reason, were not completed in childhood. However, it can sometimes be overwhelming when we do find what we long for. Fears can bubble up which lead us to sabotage or stall the progress we've begun. This may result in the dissolution of the relationship or the kind of stuck relationship described throughout this book.

Projective identification

Remarkably, we often discover that people we're attracted to turn out to have had similar life experiences. We don't know what it is that draws people who need each other together in this way, but it may be that there are very subtle signals passed between individuals which attract them. Obvious examples would be couples where both partners lost a sibling in childhood, had an alcoholic parent or had both been involved in a car crash at some point. Though such similarities are easily recognisable, they may not be discovered until *after* the couple begin bonding, suggesting unconscious processes are at work.

Far more subtle similarities may never be recognised at all. For example, though there may be no coinciding events, the way both partners experienced their childhood may be very similar. Though they may even describe it differently, both may have longed for more closeness and affection in their families, leaving them feeling not good enough, for instance. The way they've each managed these feelings, now and in the past, will interest them both and offer potential learning, so they may provoke the difficult-to-manage feeling in the other through a process known as 'projective identification'. Projective identification involves one person stimulating a response in another who is capable of this feeling and likely to respond. This explains why we're attracted to people who've had similar experiences, and is illustrated by what happened to Dom and Elaine.

Dom and Elaine

The couple were in their late fifties when they met online. Both had lost their spouse to cancer a few years previously, so they understood much of what the other was feeling. They discovered that they'd also both lost baby sons and that Dom's wife had suffered from depression more or less continuously after this. It wasn't until some months after they first met that they found out they'd also both lost their father at age ten. They thought this was an amazing series of coincidences which strengthened their growing bond.

Elaine felt very sad for Dom, who seemed to remain burdened by the misfortunes. She understood that his marriage had been disappointing. His wife had withdrawn after losing their baby, leaving him without much affection in his life, whereas she had stayed close to her husband. She also assumed that he'd missed the presence of a man after his dad died, though actually Dom hadn't been close to his father. If anything, he and his brothers had feared his dad's tempers, and their lives had improved when he died. Dom had been close to his mother, who was still alive, but who suffered from depression. He considered her weak, as she'd never protected Dom and his brothers from his dad's rages – when he would shout, hit out and break their property. Though close to his two adult daughters, Dom regretted that his baby son had died, as he'd wanted to prove to himself that dads could be different with their sons.

Dom admired the way Elaine seemed to manage her feelings and was impressed that she hadn't succumbed to depression despite all that life had thrown at her. She told him how sad she was that she'd never been able to take care of her baby and that she also felt she'd let down her parents, siblings and husband. Dom found this hard to understand as Elaine seemed so caring, but she insisted they'd all have been closer if she was somehow a better person.

Dom seemed to be testing Elaine's caring nature, frequently suggesting they watch sad movies, reading tragic stories from the newspapers and recounting heart-breaking incidents he'd heard about from friends and work colleagues, interested to see how Elaine responded. Sometimes she'd cry at the stories and films and ask Dom for a hug. She also seemed to recognise the deeper sadness in Dom and would say she could see how much these stories affected him. Whenever she thought he was sad, she would cuddle him or hold his hand tightly.

Containment

Dom felt literally 'held' by Elaine, which was a new and wonderful experience. Whatever happened, her generally calm and loving presence made him feel that all his fears and hurt were contained and neutralised. This is very similar to the experience of babies and children whose emotions are 'contained' by their carers, effectively teaching them how to manage their feelings. If you think of the emotion expressed by a crying baby who is hungry, wet or in need of a cuddle, they may seem to be expressing emotions such as fear, distress and anger. Carers often respond by using comforting 'baby talk', soothing touch and facial expressions which acknowledge the baby's feelings and suggest their needs are about to be met. The carer doesn't reproduce the baby's mental state, as this would be terrifying, but their parodying of the baby's feelings and their pacifying convey to the baby that his needs are understood. This process, illustrated in the figure on page 88, shows the effect on the baby who learns that his angry, fearful and distressed feelings can be soothed away, that they aren't harmful and that, despite his needs and emotions, he is cared for. All is well.

As he grows, the baby will learn more about affect management and start to develop self-soothing strategies, such as watching his mobile or playing with his toes while he waits for his carer. His carer's composed presence, calming talk and cuddles will help to pacify him when he's angry, hurt or frightened. Eventually, he'll be able to use self-talk to soothe himself. But imagine what happens if his carer doesn't come when he cries, treats him roughly, doesn't mirror his feelings or shows scared, angry or distressed feelings of their own. This little person may grow up without the skills to manage his mood, including his anger and distress. He may even believe his needs or emotions caused his carer's unhelpful behaviour.

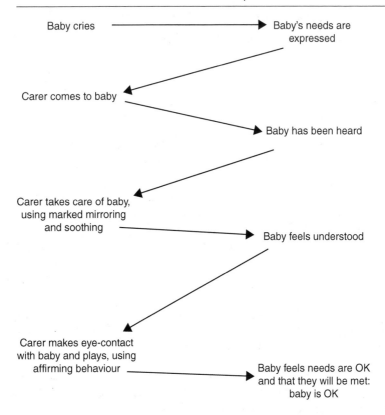

Figure 1 The origins of mood management

Dom was fairly well able to manage his feelings, but not well enough to cope with the emotions evoked by his relationship with Elaine. He was baffled by the way she managed to engage with sadness directly, whereas Dom felt that if *he* started to cry he would never ever stop. The more Dom found himself loving Elaine, the more he started pushing her away. Though he'd longed for a relationship like this, he wasn't sure how to react. He began to explore behaviour like his father's – unreasonable tempers and unnecessary sulks. He told himself that Elaine was irritating and too emotional, but he was also vaguely aware of feeling scared that if they became any closer Elaine might find out that he wasn't good enough for her and abandon him.

Meanwhile, Elaine's not-good-enough feelings were being provoked by Dom's inconsistent behaviour. She had a tendency to defer to men and feel responsible for their emotional welfare, a way of behaving she'd witnessed, and which had been expected of her, in her family and in her previous marriage. However, in neither of these were her efforts ever seen as good enough. As a result, far from abandoning Dom, she tried harder to please and care for him, as though this was what he was demanding in order to stay with her. Dom would've been amazed if he'd known this, as he felt Elaine had the upper hand and that it was only a matter of time before she rejected him.

'As if' behaviour

When they became close, Dom's fear of losing Elaine led him to treat her as though she was actually rejecting him. 'As if' behaviour, where an individual treats other people – or another person – as if they were someone else or behaving in a way they actually aren't, is known as 'transference' (see also page 53). Dom had been experiencing Elaine's kindness and care as being like the parents he wished he'd had. However, this wasn't what he was used to, as his parents and wife hadn't been as unconditionally loving as Elaine. Because he cared so much for Elaine, just as he'd cared for his parents and wife, he started to associate Elaine with the feelings of abandonment from these previous relationships, and started treating her as if she wanted to abandon him too.

Feelings of inadequacy were increasingly surfacing in Dom. He hated this and found himself provoking Elaine so that she'd defend herself, but she would often just cry and lock herself in the bathroom. Then Dom would tell her how pathetic she was – as if she was his mother whom he'd found weak and who never fought back to protect herself or her children. Attacking Elaine's 'weakness' also made Dom briefly feel stronger, as if he'd given his own weakness to her and disowned it. Dom initially didn't like this behaviour in himself, but he began to find it easy to justify as he increasingly believed it would only be a matter of time before Elaine dumped him.

Countertransference

The response to 'as if' behaviour is known as 'countertransference', when the other person actually does start behaving in the way that's been imagined. The complex form of countertransference that occurs in projective identification is the response to provocation from another person which induces behaviours and feelings. This reaction is a result of identification with the projected feeling. Dom provoked Elaine to react to upsetting stories or films in order to see how she coped with distress. Later, he provoked her to show distress and vulnerability, which satisfied Dom in three main ways:

- it reduced the intimacy between them, thereby limiting the risk of pain if Elaine abandoned him;
- it helped him to justify his unkind behaviour, which was both necessary to enact the projective identification and an emotional response to the confused and overwhelming feelings the loving relationship had produced;
- it allowed him to attack the defencelessness and hurt Elaine expressed, both aspects of himself that he intensely disliked.

Projective identification affects all relationships. Sometimes a positive emotion can be projected (such as love), but it particularly contributes to and maintains conflict. If one partner is mean and makes the other cry, for example, they can see vulnerability and unhappiness outside of themselves, which offers some temporary relief from feelings of shame and badness. These can be so disturbing that they're often split off from awareness. Thus, if someone berates their partner for an emotional response, they can enjoy even more attack on their disowned feelings, which may cause an even more passionate defence, offering yet more to attack.

People rarely do this consciously or realise how unpleasant they're being to the other partner because, fundamentally, they're attacking themselves. Moreover, this provocation often occurs during an argument, when the rational organising part of the brain is probably unavailable. It can be difficult to say who began the whole thing, especially if each partner is pressing the other's buttons, triggering defensive responses. Frequently, it's the provocation for the other partner to defend themselves which brings out the desired response. However, this only works if the partner receiving the provocation – or projection – reacts to it. For example, one partner may tell the other that they're lazy when they're clearly nothing of the sort. But if that partner fears being called lazy or has generally low self-esteem, they may react defensively, offering much to criticise. In the case of Dom and Elaine, it's possible that Elaine was also feeling confused and overwhelmed, and that some of this was somehow being projected into Dom. At some level, hurt and vulnerability may have been more acceptable to her than confusion and a sense of being overwhelmed.

Even though this toing and froing of emotions is exhausting, it's common in relationships for behavioural patterns which use projective identification to emerge and stick. This is how the same argument becomes endlessly repeated, with each partner feeling utterly trapped and unable to break free of the toxic dynamic. As soon as one partner behaves differently, however, the other will respond differently too. Ideas on how to do this can be found in Chapter 9.

Shame

Underlying the behaviours that sabotage relationships are feelings of not being good enough or shame. The way couples manage their shame or inadequacy is often played out in the kind of exchanges experienced by Dom and Elaine. Shame is a socialising concept, as it makes us want to be accepted and to conform to group norms. Mostly, we're able to manage feelings of shame, which manifest as embarrassment or regret. However, deeper feelings of not being good enough – or even bad – are often so unbearable that their management is much more difficult, especially when shame is associated with something like need or vulnerability. Interestingly, shame is not so often associated with anger, at least initially, so anger often replaces other emotions. For instance, the closer Dom and Elaine became, the more vulnerable Dom felt, but he didn't show his fear and vulnerability. Instead, he became angry.

Shame can be evoked in babies and children when their needs aren't met or when their feelings aren't appropriately mirrored, understood or attended to. So if, for instance, a child's need for comfort is derided, ignored or even punished, comfort and care becomes associated with shame. Let's say, for instance, that Dom's busy mother became angry with him when he ran to her. Maybe she told him to stop making a fuss and he continued to cry. If she was really stressed, she may have smacked him or withdrawn from him, making him feel unworthy and bad for wanting soothing. These feelings can resurface when offered love and comfort as an adult, possibly explaining Dom's extreme difficulty in accepting Elaine's care, even though this was what he longed for.

Dr Donald Nathanson (1994) identified four ways of managing not-good-enough feelings:

- Withdrawal
- Attack self
- Avoidance
- Attack other.

Using 'withdrawal', you probably try to stay out of the spotlight, maybe wishing you could disappear. In extreme cases this may mean being unable to face people at all. 'Attack self' is a similar strategy, whereby someone puts themselves down either privately or openly, perhaps using self-mocking humour. This can make the person seem 'well able to take a joke', so others may feel it's OK to tease them. Unfortunately, for some people, this may actually feel devastating. Then, what others consider to be gentle teasing seems like confirmation of their awfulness. Sometimes, people may actually self-harm.

Both the 'withdrawal' and the 'attack self' coping strategies involve conscious awareness of feeling not good enough. In 'avoidance' and 'attack other' the person has distanced themselves from the not-good-enough feelings, sometimes to the extent that they seem grandiose or super-confident.

Someone using avoidance may be able to keep their negative feelings at bay by being extremely busy – or 'driven' – and enjoying an adrenaline buzz from risky sports or activities. This can become addictive and may be associated with other behaviours that mask the unwanted feelings, such as heavy drinking, drug use, compulsive shopping, gambling or excessive use of pornography. Alternatively, or additionally, the person may show off or draw attention to their achievements. What's actually happening is that they're deflecting attention away from their negative, not-good-enough areas towards more successful aspects of themselves.

People using attack self and withdrawal often have highly perfectionist tendencies too, which can sometimes involve low tolerance for mistakes in others. The 'attack other' way of coping always involves some sort of shaming put-down and derision, often provoked by anger at any sort of snub, whether this is real or imagined, deliberate or unintentional. Some people using this strategy are not overtly critical but may use more subtle or 'passive-aggressive' tactics to unsettle people. Generally, they don't respond well to criticism themselves and don't accept blame or responsibility.

As attack self and withdrawal are within conscious awareness, they're easier to change and less likely to affect other people, though those using them may feel very bad about themselves. The attack other and avoidance strategies are much harder to change, as they're outside conscious awareness and may not feel like a problem to anyone who employs them. However, they may affect relationships, as others feel criticised or that the relationship is unequal. Compulsive behaviours or relationship issues are consequently what often bring people to counselling rather than an awareness of not feeling good enough. Unfortunately, the kind of soothing relationship needed in order to let go of these strategies is unlikely to develop because of them. This, in itself, may trigger not-good-enough feelings which have to be defended against, so that the attack other and avoidance behaviours become intensified.

Shame triggers

Looking back at your previous relationship, you may be able to identify the use of these strategies in fights with your partner. It's not hard to imagine how each partner could trigger the other to use their own shame management strategies. For instance, a partner who withdraws may remind the other of a parent who refused to speak to them. This is a behaviour management strategy that has great potential for damage, as young children are unable to cope with their feelings while a carer is withdrawn. Consequently, one partner withdrawing because they don't feel good enough, or simply to allow some space for recovery and reflection, can result in the other experiencing the withdrawal as punishing or rejecting and defending themselves by attack.

Something similar happened with Dom and Elaine, but in their case Elaine eventually looked for change. At a time when they weren't arguing, she sat Dom down and told him she couldn't understand what had happened, as she'd been so happy with Dom. Elaine was very clear that she wanted to be with Dom and would do anything she could to reassure him of this – but she couldn't continue the way they were. Dom appeared relieved, apologised and tried to be different, but he still found himself sometimes picking on Elaine. Instead of being upset and retaliating, Elaine usually managed to ask Dom if he needed some quiet time and to tell him that she was going to give him some space until he felt better. Gradually, this became Dom's cue to calm down. He started to believe that Elaine really did love him and wasn't going to leave – unless he pushed her away.

Not all couples have the mental reserves to find their own solutions, and this one did rely on Elaine containing Dom's feelings until he was able to do this for himself. Individual or couple therapy could have helped them resolve their issues more quickly. Seeking outside help is definitely advisable in relationships where there's volatility. As well as emotional damage, there's always a risk that a row could get out of hand and spill over into violence or damage to property. Ideally, both partners should be able to manage their feelings and to support one another in doing this. Often, one partner takes emotional responsibility for the relationship, as Elaine did, but this unbalances the couple and can drain the responsible partner to the point where their love just ebbs away. In couples where neither partner has the emotional reserves to contain the other's shame and vulnerability, the couple endlessly trigger each other's pain and are unable to escape from their toxic dance.

Dom and Elaine, however, ended the collusive dynamic in which they were unconsciously acting out and replaying earlier unresolved experiences from their lives. Elaine's brave refusal to continue their painful and unhealthy collusion enabled them both to accomplish the psychological changes they'd longed for. Dom had never before achieved the closeness or validation of his feelings that Elaine provided, and Elaine for the first time provided good-enough care that was appreciated and valued. Chapter 7 explores further what happens when unfinished business continues to be unresolved.

Remember: The complementary roles developed by couples often work well. Even collusive relationships like Dom and Elaine's can work effectively to keep their fears – such as intimacy, loss of identity or rejection – at bay. However, collusion can prevent couples from achieving aspects of their relationship that have been missing from their lives and stall personal development.

Bibliography

Jenkins, H. (2006) Inside out, or outside in: Meeting with couples. *Journal of Family Therapy*, 28, 113–135.

Nathanson, D. L. (1994) *Shame and Pride: Affect, Sex and the Birth of the Self*, New York: Norton.

Chapter 7

Unfinished business

We saw in the last chapter how unresolved issues can continue to influence the way we think and behave. This, in turn, affects how we deal with more recent hurts and losses and whether we're able to find a place for any of them in the story of our lives. Our ways of behaving aren't something we necessarily plan or are aware of, and some of the traumas we've experienced aren't consciously remembered, even though they can still affect us. This may be something that concerns you as you enter a new relationship. If, for instance, previous abuse affects your sexual expression, if you've never recovered from the loss of someone close or if you have mental health issues, you may be apprehensive about this affecting your new relationship, especially if it's been a problem in relationships before.

Knowing when or whether to talk to your partner about whatever this is can be tricky. You might not want to suggest you have a ton of baggage, but equally know it would help to be prepared. Before you agree to any major commitments, it's useful to have a conversation or two, construed as planning rather than confessional, about aspects of your life that could trip you *both* up. This initial, and probably tentative, conversation will give you both permission to address whatever might bother you going forward.

Unfortunately, many of us refuse to admit even to ourselves that past events may be responsible for, or contributing to, some of our current issues. However, not acknowledging this makes them all the more powerful, particularly if their effects turn out to be triggered by the new relationship or aspects of that partner's life. If you know you sometimes become moody, angry or withdrawn, say, it makes sense to discuss how to manage this when it happens.

Unresolved grief

Unfinished business produces grief and there's nothing like losing a partner or going through a painful divorce for triggering a whole lot more. It's common to be unaware that grief has become chronic, particularly if you've worked hard to keep going and tried to remain unaffected. Many of us apparently cope well with terrible events at the time, only for some minor incident to set off a major reaction long afterwards.

Unresolved grief can become cumulative. Left unexpressed, it's out of the control you've sought to exert over it, a burden waiting to bite. Ironically, it's often when life settles that the space for chronic grief becomes available, and can sometimes just hit you at a time when life seems perfect. In fact, the better your new relationship, the more likely it is that you'll relax enough to find yourself unexpectedly facing whatever it is you've been avoiding. As well as the very obvious issue of your former partner, this may include:

- abuse or neglect
- accidents or injuries
- adoption
- bereavement and loss
- bullying
- difficulty with education or exams
- drug or alcohol problems
- effects of previous relationship(s)
- financial problems
- gambling
- identity issues and coming out
- infertility
- moving home or housing problems
- ongoing family conflict
- parents with problems
- physical or mental health problems for yourself or a family member
- problems with children
- problems with the law
- problems with work
- sexual problems
- step-family issues.

It's likely that at least a few of the listed issues, and possibly many more, will have affected you. Not only is this list a mere taste of potential challenges, but it doesn't take into account all the forgotten or unacknowledged very early traumas and losses each partner brings to a relationship. Even remembered childhood trauma may not be recognised as such, especially when it was chronic, yet it may produce much unfinished business, as we saw with Dom and Elaine in Chapter 6. Disappointment and loss within relationships also accumulate into grief, particularly when couples are unable to express how they're affected. It's worth pausing to reflect on how you've dealt with the issues on your own list. Also consider how helpful your partner was, if you had one at the time, what may still be affecting you and what you may need to do now. The quiz below may help to give you an idea of how open you are to past hurts, though if you really don't want to know about them you probably won't do the quiz!

Quiz: How in touch with the past are you?

1. Your new partner asks questions about school and growing up. Do you:
    a) Remember it quite well and relate some stories, good and bad.
    b) Remember very well, but doing so is sometimes upsetting.
    c) Remember hardly anything before your teens.
    d) Remember quite well, but there are some gaps.
2. Which one of the following applies most to you?
    a) You have happy and sad memories.
    b) You're aware of some very bad memories.
    c) Your memories are largely happy.
    d) You occasionally have flashbacks.
3. When do you mostly talk about the past?
    a) When reminiscing with family and friends.
    b) When you're upset.
    c) As an anecdote, to entertain.
    d) You rarely discuss the past.
4. When you tell stories about the past, you:
    a) Sometimes misremember a detail or two.
    b) Find your memory jumps about from one event to another.
    c) Tell well-honed and well-received stories.
    d) Ramble a bit.

5. Which is usually the most important element of your memories to get across to others?
    a) It depends on the memory and who you're talking to.
    b) Your feelings or how you were treated.
    c) Its entertainment value.
    d) Depends on what the other person wants to know.
6. How do you usually feel when talking about the past?
    a) It depends on the memory.
    b) Upset and often that you're not being heard.
    c) Quite good, as the stories generally go down well.
    d) Confused.
7. Are the memories you relate:
    a) A mixture of triumphs and embarrassments.
    b) Often quite blaming.
    c) Usually centred on yourself.
    d) Often self-deprecating or awkward.
8. What happens to your most painful memories?
    a) I don't avoid painful memories but try to balance them with happy ones.
    b) They crop up a lot.
    c) I'm quite good at compartmentalising.
    d) I try not to think about them.

Mostly As

You probably have quite good access to your memories and mostly enjoy looking back. Though there may be some which are sad or upsetting, you do still allow them.

Mostly Bs

In general, you have an excellent memory and can access considerable detail. You probably have some quite painful memories which are difficult to talk about but that you very much want to share. You may feel people don't always understand what you're relating, but you feel it's important to get your point across and don't mind talking about the past.

Mostly Cs

You probably remember themes from your childhood rather than specific memories. You're good at putting unpleasant memories behind you and focusing on happier times. You may be a good storyteller, making the most of incidents in your life to entertain others.

Mostly Ds

Some of your memories may be vague and you may be unsure about their accuracy. Other people who were there may describe events differently, which adds to this impression. Some memories may take you by surprise or you may have occasional flashbacks or nightmares about the past.

Body scanning

If you feel you may need to address some issues from your past, it can be useful to tune in to your body, as awareness of somatic changes can help you to recognise the triggers for connections. Scanning your body from top to toe when you're calm should help you to recognise your body's baseline. You could keep a note, or even a journal, to try to notice when you have more troubled sensations. Some people have great difficulty in recognising bodily feelings and may need to concentrate very hard to do so. Lying down and focusing first on your breathing may be helpful, unless you experience health anxiety, when this sort of concentration on your body may make you feel worse. Otherwise, changes you're looking for include:

- dizziness
- headache
- dry mouth
- joint, limb or neck tension or pain
- sweatiness
- tight chest
- butterflies
- trembling or feeling wobbly
- tingling extremities
- frequently needing the loo.

It can be useful to note what you were doing or thinking just before you spotted any changes in bodily sensations. If you practise body scanning regularly, you'll notice the changes earlier and be able to distract yourself before you start feeling really bad. If you can note the thoughts, emotions and behaviour that occur with the bodily feelings, you may recognise common themes. This helps to pinpoint triggers that evoke feelings or memories, and you may even be able to see how they link to the past and the unfinished business that needs addressing before you'll feel better. Some people can go right through triggering episodes without noticing their bodies at all. They might even attribute their change in mood to the attention their irritability provokes. Such failure to recognise mood triggers can affect relationships negatively, as you *both* misattribute what's happening.

Felt memories

Body scanning may be especially helpful in recognising the memories that are experienced as emotions. These are associated with the period before speech development or from times when you've frozen during some sort of trauma. These 'felt' memories seem current, which can be lovely if they give you a warm comforting feeling, but anything from unsettling to terrifying if they provoke anxiety. Panic attacks may be a type of felt memory, as they often come out of nowhere and seem to have no point.

You need to take special care of yourself if you start dealing with unresolved grief or trauma by yourself. Ideally, you'll do this with the help of a psychotherapist or counsellor, but sometimes memories just crowd in unexpectedly and can be very disturbing. Do seek help and inform your general practitioner (GP) if this is troubling or interfering with your life, especially if you're having panic attacks, flashbacks or any thoughts of self-harm. Eye movement desensitisation and reprocessing (EMDR) is a relatively recent intervention, developed by American psychologist Francine Shapiro, which processes memories so that they become less troubling. Accredited therapists can be found through the European EMDR Association (http://emdrassociation.org.uk/profile/members-2).

Pain and stress

Sometimes, a perfectly lovely second relationship is marred by the unexpected emergence of pain from earlier times, or there are continuing issues that eat away at your wellbeing. Equally, a current relationship in which you've tolerated a great deal may buckle. This could have nothing to do with relationship quality, but be related to how much the relationship has had to endure. Trying to just power through pain only works up to a point. Sometimes it's essential to take a breath and consider what you need to do to recover from so much accumulated distress. This is particularly the case if you and your partner deal with what's happening separately, rather than acknowledging your stress and managing it as a team.

Life events frequently contribute to the development of disappointment and chronic grief, perhaps even more so if the individuals involved feel ashamed or that they aren't coping well enough. The way we've been brought up undoubtedly affects the way we manage stresses. For instance, one partner may discourage discussion of problems, assuming that staying strong and apparently unaffected is a way of supporting the other, who meanwhile desperately needs to get things off their chest. Hence, a major problem for many relationships affected by external events is the way each partner thinks they should be attended to.

One partner often feels strongly that the other should manage their ex-partner/children/in-laws/parents/depression/alcohol abuse and so on in a particular way that doesn't work for them. For instance, many couples don't agree about the way children are disciplined or indulged, or become anxious when a partner gets on with their ex. If the issue starts defining the relationship, matters of loyalty and pride kick in to exacerbate the problem. Though these concerns have their roots in the past, they can affect the here and now in a very real way. They're then often linked to current arguments over issues such as childcare, sexual frequency, finances, holidays, how to do family visits, how to load the dishwasher... Disputes are triggered, often leading to development of no-go areas. Now loneliness may be added to the stresses affecting you both.

Though it's rarely helpful for a couple to disagree about everything, relationships don't thrive if you agree about everything either. Difference is essential or there can be no relationship. There will inevitably be some issues you'll never agree on. If this really bothers you, spend some time thinking about what it is that upsets you about having different points of view. Understanding each other's differences is halfway to a solution. Though agreement is great, there still needs to be room for individuality and ability for the relationship to manage the intrusion of other ideas and needs that may be expressed too – such as those of family, children, colleagues and friends.

Blended families

Children from previous relationships are a constant reminder that your partner has had a life without you. While some people enjoy stories about their partner's past, others find them threatening, perhaps because what's happened can't be changed. Some people then not only avoid talking about the past but also steer clear of anyone who shared that past. This accounts for some of the problems experienced with in-laws and, particularly, with a partner's children. It's easy to find fault with young children and teenagers, especially as they may initially be wary or worry you don't like them. They have no more idea how to behave in this new situation than you do, so the easiest way may be to ignore you. You may then think they don't like you, and either ignore them too or try too hard to get their attention, when what they need is space to adjust. It helps to keep initial meetings brief and to build up the time you spend together gradually.

Partners can assume you'll get on because they expect that the people they love the most will automatically love each other. They need to understand that the children also love the ex-partner, may feel that to even like you compromises their loyalty, and that meeting you makes the split real. If they're grieving, it's even more important to be sensitive. Children don't behave in binary, predictable ways and don't necessarily have the cognitive skills to understand, let alone explain, their mixed emotions. Confusingly, the more they like you, the more they may be disagreeable if they feel guilty about getting on with you so well.

Often, your partner's children will love spending time with you and care for you very deeply. Some have a rough time with their partner's ex if they're very upset and bitter about the split and using their children as confidantes. If they have to be too grown up, your new family may offer some light relief from their other life and a chance to relax. This doesn't mean you have to accept terrible behaviour, but neither does it mean you can behave badly. Nor does it mean it's acceptable for your children to bully or belittle your partner's kids or for them to pick on yours. If this happens, make it clear that it isn't OK, but don't react with too many restrictions and punishment which just reinforce existing negative beliefs. Instead, it helps to create some happy times where everyone enjoys themselves. If possible, try some activities that are new to you all. Or if you or your partner have a particular skill, try sharing it.

You're likely to have different rules and ways of going about things, which your partner's children won't necessarily pick up on. These have to be explained, and you and your partner need to be consistent about them. Asking the ex for advice about the children's needs is always likely to be helpful. They'll probably be grateful and reassured to be consulted, and find it much harder to create difficulties if you're reasonable and friendly. If you mind that your partner gets on with his ex, bear in mind that this will make *your* life much easier than it would be if your partner were constantly being upset by them. The ex is also more likely to encourage the children to get on with you if they do.

Make sure that your partner has enough time alone with their children, especially when you're first together. It may be a strain for all of you trying to get on, so you may all appreciate the downtime this provides. It's also important that children continue to do whatever made their relationship with your partner special. For instance, imagine what it would be like to have your special weekend treat shared with a stranger – awkward all round and very disappointing for the child. Bear in mind, too, that you and your partner have the rest of your lives together, but the few precious years of childhood can pave the way for you all to have a great relationship in the many more years when they're grown up. Alternatively, you could set yourself up for decades of resentment and, potentially, for the children to learn that their needs aren't recognised or important. Indeed, troubled family relationships are at the heart of much of the 'baggage' we carry and which remains unaddressed.

Recognising grief

It's tragic that couples and families may stifle feelings of disappointment, grief and loss, and misunderstand each other's way of expressing these to the extent that they remain latent for decades. All hopes and dreams can be elusive when it comes to explaining to others, and even to oneself, what has been lost. For couples, this can be exacerbated by a belief that romance can and should be enough to deal with life's struggles. Therefore, anything less than an idyllic life is considered unacceptable, so that partners start to see themselves or the relationship as failing (Reibstein, 2006). This can have a circular effect, as the more our sense of identity and our expectations are compromised by events and disappointments, the more likely we are to experience intense and lasting grief (Keesee et al., 2008).

Failure to express distress, and to create meaningful narratives which explain and make sense of what's happened, allows grief to not only linger but feed upon itself. It's normal to go over and over a trauma in your mind for a few weeks afterwards, a process that eventually lets what happened settle into your long-term memory where it becomes faded and more manageable. People who don't do this often experience longer effects, sometimes even developing post-traumatic stress disorder years later (Van der Kolk, 2015). Stress from childhood can make people hypervigilant and wary, some even living as adults with attention deficit disorder (Crittenden et al., 2014).

Talking

Discourses around keeping going, putting loss behind us and staying strong encourage people not to discuss their pain. Even when they do, the way the conversations take place may not be enough in themselves to allow resolution of painful feelings (Hooghe et al., 2011). It's important to try to work out what you need, and not assume you *should* feel better, soldiering on when you're actually still suffering. How much conversations allow the expression of grief and meaning-making usually depends on beliefs about the benefits of the process and ability to tolerate distress. Frequently, people believe they shouldn't talk in case it involves being upset, or one closes the other down when they cry. However, without tears and going over the event many times, pain remains. However hard you try to ignore it, it lurks in short-term memory, current and dangerous.

Many people hide their pain from others if past experience leads them to expect their own needs or distress are subjects to be avoided. Consequently, beliefs about others' expectations of how grief and distress ought to be performed can close down their authentic expression. Sometimes talking is avoided because it really does make someone feel much worse, whereas avoidance helps. This is often a matter of timing and the way comfort is offered. Productive conversations often don't feel possible at the time of a distressing event, when attention, acknowledgement of pain and care can be more helpful. However, by the time talk feels possible, there may be no one to listen. Others may seem to assume you're over the event and moving on. This may be just your perception or others may genuinely be wary of reigniting your pain. This puts the onus on you to make clear your needs, but many of us believe that only a sunny disposition is acceptable and never get the chance to express what we've been through.

Displacement

The more intangible the cause of grief, the more difficult it may be to grieve effectively (Cudmore, 2005). Infertility is an example of intangible loss as there is no person to mourn. Miscarriage is another example of distress that some people, particularly men, think should be endured privately or even considered not enough to cause grief (Nazaré et al., 2012). Sometimes, a partner may end the relationship, start an affair or otherwise unconsciously create a distraction that becomes the focus of grief, rather than the actual painful event, because it appears to be a more valid reason to be upset.

Many men *and* women believe men aren't comforted by talking about loss, whereas women tend to actively seek support from partner, family and friends and to find talking helps them. Men's reluctance to talk may, therefore, result from fear of distressing their partner, fear of being distressed by their partner and/or belief that they need to be the 'strong' member of the couple. It isn't just that some men hide or repress their feelings; men are not always given a chance to express their grief. In addition to being silenced by the belief that others expect them not to want to talk, many people – not just men – don't know how to start an important or tricky conversation.

In relationships, problems occur particularly when one partner's reluctance to talk is interpreted as not caring or the other's need to talk is rejected, yet the way each partner needs to grieve or express pain may never have been explored. Relying on assumptions to guide you where there is stress, pain or grief is unlikely to hit the spot. It's the ability to discover and accept the way the other copes that fosters intimacy and recovery (Korenromp et al., 2007) and ultimately helps to create a shared approach.

However, couples of either gender often collude to displace their feelings, putting energy into work, childcare and so on. These unconscious attempts to smother grief can actually exacerbate pain and disappointment. When unfinished business is lurking, and there seems to be no focus for their feelings, couples are inclined to blame each other for their distress rather than the event. Sometimes, this facilitates the necessary difficult conversations, which generate more fruitful understanding. Often, though, it produces a recurring complaint that remains unresolved until the pain from the actual event is addressed. One partner's inability to meet the needs of the other in a time of difficulty is often a trigger. Jenna's partner, Jim, for example, went to a football match the day after Jenna's father died. From Jim's point of view, other family members were with Jenna and he stuck by her side for the rest of the weekend. Jenna, though, felt hugely hurt, and this pain seemed bigger than the loss of her dad.

Looking back at previous relationships now, you may be able to see your own or your partner's reluctance to share distress as contributing to your problems. If so, it's all the more important to make an effort to communicate how you're feeling in your subsequent relationships. It can also be helpful in a new relationship to identify trigger areas that could provide a deal-breaker. For instance, if affairs, financial problems or addictions affected your previous relationship, or even the relationship of your parents, a sibling or close friend, you may be especially alert for these. Difficulties with trust, secrecy over money or commenting on your partner's drinking, gambling or shopping habits may be the result. A partner who feels you have no reason to be concerned may be perplexed, insulted or even angry if you seem unnecessarily focused on issues they're convinced are no threat. They need to know and understand that you're not over the hurt they caused and that your terror is that it could happen again. Being clear about what bothers you is as important as being able to empathise and take your feelings into account.

Depression

Depression is sometimes related to unresolved events or traumas, but it can just happen and be unfinished business in itself. Depression can have a negative effect on relationships, and it may be difficult to determine whether a relationship is causing depression or whether it's the other way round. If you have a history of depression, you may hope that your new relationship will prevent this in future. If you do then become depressed, disappointment may mean you blame your relationship, however supportive or understanding your partner may be.

Some people put a great deal of pressure on themselves to live up to an impossible image. Depression and/or anxiety may then be a reaction to feeling they aren't fulfilling their own or others' expectations of them within a new relationship. This may be especially the case in those juggling the competing demands of, for instance, their former family, ex-partner, parents, children, new partner and work. It's easy to feel pulled in all directions, unable to meet the needs of anyone.

Those who feel they ought to be able to overcome their depression, and who refuse help, generally prolong their illness and distress others. Men often try to hide emotional problems (Wittenborn et al., 2012), so their depression may emerge not as sadness but as anger, irritability, sleep difficulties, sexual problems, increased alcohol use, working more, ill-health and denying there's anything wrong! Unfortunately, this can push partners away, creating or increasing dissatisfaction with the relationship. It's helpful to discuss what should happen if either of you become low or ill, particularly if you've had problems previously. Shutting your partner out will only make matters worse, however, and can actually lead to them becoming depressed too.

Vikram and Lily

Vikram believed his partner Lily would interpret his depression as weakness, so didn't share how he was feeling nor tell her that he had experienced bouts of depression for most of his life. Lily saw Vikram's moodiness, irritability and withdrawal as rejection of her. She felt very hurt and began to ruminate on what it could be about her that was making Vikram behave in this way. She was afraid to mention her concerns to Vikram in case he took the opportunity to end the relationship. She also started to worry about the future and what would happen if Vikram left her, becoming more and more anxious. Meanwhile, Vikram assumed her irritability and low mood were rejecting of him, which he imagined was due to Lily's disgust about his depression. By this time, the relationship – which had been perfectly happy beforehand – was in serious trouble, which could have been avoided if only there had been more openness about their concerns.

Recovery

It can be unhelpful to just return to normal when a depressed person starts to feel a little better. It's easy to fall into the trap of avoiding any mention of depression if you aren't sure how to approach it, but this doesn't mean you can't check on your partner's overall wellbeing and make a point of expressing interest in how they are. For some people, not having their needs and feelings acknowledged causes their depression, so how they are needs to be monitored even when they seem fine again. Nonetheless, it isn't helpful to completely take over a depressed partner's care and responsibilities as this just leaves them feeling incapable and dependent. Encouragement to attempt activities and tasks can be very helpful, especially when the effort is appreciated.

Co-operating is always more helpful to the relationship than when each partner works entirely separately on an issue, effectively shutting out the other. If Vikram had explained to Lily that he suffered from depression and needed more time to himself, it's likely that she'd have given it freely. She'd probably have been a little more solicitous as well, though the couple could have negotiated how they managed the depression on an ongoing basis. Vikram would have derived considerable comfort from snuggling up on the sofa with Lily, but he felt ashamed to do this and scared that Lily might ask awkward questions about his wellbeing if they were too close.

Vulnerability

Being able to have conversations about difficult issues often requires a fundamental shift in attitude, such as starting to believe that it's acceptable to have low moods and needs and to sometimes be vulnerable. First of all, you have to realise that you're behaving according to a set of rules for yourself that you may not even be aware of. The questions below are useful with any feeling states – love, care, anger, hurt and rejection are especially interesting to explore. However, let's start with the feeling of vulnerability.

- What makes me feel vulnerable?
- What do I do when I feel vulnerable – for example, withdraw, avoid the feeling, seek comfort from someone close, be angry...?
- Who can I talk to about feeling vulnerable?
- Is feeling vulnerable acceptable?
- What rules do I have about feeling vulnerable?
- What are my beliefs about feeling vulnerable?
- How do others react to my vulnerability?
- How would they know that what I'm showing is vulnerability?

The last question is crucial, as partners may be responding to the anger you show rather than to the underlying feeling. If one of your rules about vulnerability is that it isn't to be shown, and if you believe that it puts people off or that it's dangerous to yourself or others, it's unlikely that you'll allow it to surface authentically. An example of showing authentic vulnerability would be to say, 'Ouch, that hurt' when a comment seems unkind. Instead, many of us would respond with an attack on the person, thereby justifying to them their cruel remark.

Online triggers

Ex-partners frequently seem to be a major cause of distress long after a relationship has ended, often because there's unfinished business. After a period of intensity, parting may leave either partner with feelings of frustration if they never achieved a hoped-for outcome. If, for instance, the ex never apologised for their bad behaviour during the relationship, never paid back money they owed or never recognised the other's feelings, there may be considerable unresolved resentment and pain. Social media can be used to inflict more pain or to torture ourselves, particularly as this can trigger all sorts of past hurts. We may try to create the perfect image of our new life on Instagram, Facebook or Snapchat, just in the hope that the ex will see them. We may also want to impress friends and family and make them think we're doing better than the ex. Obviously, this is exhausting and quite depressing if you don't really feel as happy as your online profile suggests.

Checking your ex-partner's apps can be tempting. Seeing that your ex is getting on with their life may be reassuring if you're worried about them or they've been finding it hard to separate. But before you do check, consider what you want to get out of this. Do you want reassurance or just to prove that your partner is lonely and miserable? Absence of posts doesn't necessarily mean they're moping; they may be too busy to post. So do you want to make *yourself* feel lonely and miserable, to work yourself up and ruin your day by stalking them online?

A common annoyance is to see your ex apparently spending money after telling you they're broke. However, if it winds you up to see them, don't look. Blocking them may feel like a surprisingly positive move, as it'll liberate you from both the need to look at their accounts and the need to perform in your own. If you care enough about your partner's feelings to be bothered that they'll feel rejected if you block them, just mute their account so that you don't receive notifications about them.

You may also want to delete them from instant messaging apps, as these allow online presence to be seen. You can, again, mute your ex or message without showing you're online, but this may be inconvenient if others want to contact you. Some boundaries about how you and your ex will stay in touch – only by phone, e-mail or text, for instance – should avoid complaints (see also Chapter 2).

You may also want some boundaries around the way you and your new partner deal with online messaging. Awareness of online presence makes some couples upset if they feel their partner is speaking to someone else. This can also make partners feel a bit checked up on or controlled so, once again, it may be better not to keep looking. Messages themselves can be used to convey displeasure, say, by leaving off kisses or not replying. Waiting a long time to reply can be upsetting to those in whom it triggers a painful memory. As very early memories usually surface as an emotion rather than as a formed thought, it's common to attribute distress just to the message rather than also to what it's evoked – which may be beyond conscious awareness. Once again, the potential is there for misunderstanding, providing yet another aspect of our lives that needs to be talked about with partners.

Qualities

Communication is best in couples who are each able to give, take and ask for what they need to help understand each other and negotiate. For this to work, you need to be able to tolerate difference between yourself and your partner, including the way they think, their beliefs and their personal culture. If you look back at your previous relationship(s), you may be able to see how simple misunderstandings led to major problems.

Even if you bring what you see as a problem to the relationship, try not to think of it as just your issue. So long as it affects the relationship, it's a joint matter. For the future, seeing problems as external factors that can be jointly addressed will mean you both feel supported and share responsibility for their management. Two heads being better than one, you stand more chance of solving or coping with problems if you're communicating well and seeing the issues as separate to you both, rather than defining one of you.

In order to jointly tackle issues that affect the relationship, it's helpful to be able to recognise the different skills and strengths you each bring as a result of your different experiences and upbringing. The following exercise is a good way to identify how to do this.

Exercise: Qualities

1. Think of a problem you've dealt with together in the past.
2. Identify how you did this and what each partner contributed.
3. Use the Qualities Table below to help you identify qualities that each of you used on this occasion, noting how they were helpful.
4. Now consider your current problem, looking at how the qualities you've identified could be used to help this time.
5. Are there any other qualities that would help you? Which of you is more likely to possess each of them?

Qualities Table

Adventurousness	Appreciation	Bravery	Capability
Confidence	Consideration	Co-operation	Creativity
Curiosity	Enjoyment	Enthusiasm	Fairness
Faith	Focus	Forgiveness	Gratitude
Honesty	Honour	Hope	Humility
Humour	Independence	Integrity	Intimacy
Joy	Judgement	Kindness	Leadership
Love	Love of learning	Passion	Patience
Perseverance	Perspective	Positivity	Prudence
Purpose	Resourcefulness	Self-regulation	Sharing
Social skills	Spirituality	Strength	Teamwork
Tolerance	Understanding	Willingness	Zest

Lindsay and Helena

Lindsay found herself feeling jealous whenever Helena met up with her adult daughter, Kim, or when she came to visit. She felt this was silly and that Kim was no threat, so she didn't mention how she felt. Lindsay came from a competitive family who were always vying for the attention of her mother, so she wondered if this had something to do with it. Whatever it was, she found herself feeling really out of sorts and grumpy whenever Kim was mentioned, which led to arguments. Eventually, she and Lindsay used the Qualities Exercise to help them.

1. Helena realised that she used to feel very similar when Lindsay stayed late at work.
2. Lindsay remembered that they were able to deal with that when Helena admitted that Lindsay being late home triggered trust issues. On this occasion, Lindsay had been able to reassure Helena that she was genuinely working late. She'd invited Helena to call or text if she was worrying. Helena had been concerned that she'd worry more if Lindsay was too busy to reply at once, so Helena and Lindsay had thought of ways Helena could distract herself and what self-talk she could use to reassure herself.
3. The couple thought Lindsay had used *understanding, consideration* and *tolerance* in realising how affected Helena was, and that they'd both used *creativity* and *resourcefulness* in thinking about a solution. Helena had also used *self-regulation* in developing and actually using self-talk to calm herself when she was worrying about Lindsay being late.
4. When Lindsay admitted how she was feeling about Kim, the couple thought similar qualities were needed with this issue too. They agreed Lindsay was better at *understanding, consideration* and *tolerance* but that Lindsay needed these qualities, plus *trust* and *faith*, to overcome her discomfort about Kim and understand why it was so important for Helena to see her.
5. Helena also suggested that Lindsay needed *perspective* to develop self-talk so she could regulate her feelings when she became upset about Kim.

Their conversation was not entirely smooth. Helena had become a little impatient with Lindsay's moods and lack of trust, but she appreciated her willingness to try to distract herself, understand Helena's point of view and regulate her feelings. Lindsay hadn't previously wanted to spend time with Kim but they agreed it would be helpful if Lindsay could get to know Kim better, and would start by just having the occasional coffee or drink with her.

If this sort of exercise seems a little clunky, bear in mind that its awkwardness demonstrates that you're making changes. The point in preventing repetition of old mistakes is to find different ways of thinking and behaving, which means sometimes stepping outside your comfort zone. This will become even more evident in the next section of the book, which begins by looking at how to manage uncertainty.

Remember: Many of us bring unfinished business to our new relationships which we may not be fully aware of. Identifying potentially unresolved issues and discussing how to approach them can help to prevent misunderstandings and prepare for their possible impact.

Bibliography

Crittenden, P., Dallos, R., Landini, A. and Kozlowska, K. (2014) *Attachment and Family Therapy*, Maidenhead: Open University Press.

Cudmore, L. (2005) Becoming parents in the context of loss. *Sexual & Relationship Therapy*, 20(3), 299–308.

Hooghe, A. N., Neimeyer, R. A. and Rober, P. (2011) The complexity of couple communication in bereavement: An illustrative case study. *Death Studies*, 35, 905–924.

Keesee, N. J., Currier, J. M. and Neimeyer, R. A. (2008) Predictors of grief following the death of one's child: The contribution of finding meaning. *Journal of Clinical Psychology*, 134, 648–661.

Korenromp, M. J., Page-Christiaens, G. C. M. L., van den Bout, J., Mulder, E. J. H., Hunfeld, J. A. M. and Potters, C. M. A. A. (2007) A prospective study on parental coping four months after termination of pregnancy for fetal anomalies. *Prenatal Diagnosis*, 27, 709–716.

Nazaré, B., Fonseca, A. and Canavarro, C. (2012) Grief following termination of pregnancy for fetal abnormality: Does marital intimacy foster short-term couple congruence? *Journal of Reproductive and Infant Psychology*, 30(2), 168–179.

Reibstein, J. (2006) *The Best Kept Secret: Men's and Women's Stories of Lasting Love*, New York: Bloomsbury.

Van der Kolk, B. (2015) *The Body Keeps the Score*, London: Penguin Random House.

Wittenborn, A. K., Culpepper, B. and Liu, T. (2012) Treating depression in men: The role of emotionally focused couple therapy. *Contemporary Family Therapy*, 34, 89–103.

Part III

Managing new relationships

Chapter 8

Uncertainty

Conquering fear of uncertainty is a big ask at a time in your life when some certainty may be all you want. It's completely understandable to seek reassurance at the end of a long relationship or when embarking on a new one. However, fears about change or ambiguity can make us more inflexible in our thinking and behaviour, meaning we may be more likely to repeat past mistakes. Being open to new ways of thinking and behaving can only increase the range of options you have and give you more ways of managing difficulties. Indeed, being able to manage uncertainty is often the key to making relationships work. For example, if you feel OK in yourself, your partner's bad mood won't throw you off course in the way it would if you rely on their approval.

The way we speak to each other influences our view of both the other person and of ourselves. Every single exchange we have changes the relationship a little. We infer meaning from the way we're spoken to and how often, as well as the content. The way we speak positions the person we speak to as well. For instance, when we snap or seem irritable, the other person may feel put down and hurt, assume they've done something wrong or feel affronted and angry. The intention may not have been to cause hurt at all but, once done, the response comes from what the person feels was intended rather than what was actually meant.

If we made more effort to check meaning, we could create more certainty in our lives. Instead, we tend to cling more rigidly to the existing ideas and assumed meanings we know. Though this *appears* to offer security, it actually does the opposite. Then the more insecure we feel, the more obstinate we often become, even perpetuating unsafe and unhelpful relationship dynamics, such as toxic arguing, because it's familiar.

Most of us are unaware that we do any of this, making it difficult to change without really making an effort. Voices from the past also influence our thinking and behaviour, offering a sense of comfort and certainty, without which the world would be more threatening. However, this means we may be constantly trying to position others to behave in ways that we find reassuring. Inevitably, this leads to relationship clashes.

Psychologist Taibi Kahler (1975) identified five drivers that provide the underlying motivation for many of us. These drivers are derived from messages received early in life which influence the way we live:

- Be perfect
- Be strong
- Hurry up
- Please others
- Try hard.

At first glance, these drivers appear to be based on beneficial qualities. However, being governed by just one or two of these drivers can result in extremes of behaviour which are hard for the doer to manage and for others to understand, again often resulting in relationship difficulties.

Be perfect

Perfectionist tendencies underlie a great deal of anxiety and need for certainty. People who believe they must be perfect often behave as though they're being judged, and treat others as though they're judging them too. They often accuse partners of 'not helping' or 'pressurising' them when the partner would actually prefer them to be less meticulous. However, a less perfectionist partner may be thought to reflect badly on the perfectionist one, who'll nag and cajole the family to live up to their impossible standards in the way they dictate. Of course, if anyone ever did come anywhere near to doing so, they'd threaten the perfection of the perfectionist one. Consequently, such couples end up in constant competition, often trying to catch one another out.

Perfectionist partners may also find it difficult to leave work or to finish a job, as they're always finessing. This means such couples have barely any quality time. Perfectionists often say they can't relax until everything's done, and then blame everyone else for not helping them. If they do ever stop, they're too exhausted to appreciate time with their partner and family.

If this sounds like you, it's worth thinking about the impression you're creating. Far from being appreciated for being so amazing, you're probably alienating everyone close to you with your nagging and high-octane activity. Your family's memories will be of you complaining or just not being there when they wanted and needed you. That's far from perfect.

Be strong

People with this driver often come from families where emotions aren't encouraged. Happy faces are preferred and negative feelings are kept inside as much as possible. Tears may be seen as a sign of weakness and avoided. This can cause problems in relationships if, in being strong during times of trouble, the strong partner appears not to care. Strong partners also often dislike what they see as neediness, so they won't tolerate it in others and are either poor at accepting help or behave as though they're entitled to it. The rule generally, though, is to 'just get on with it' or withdraw from others, which can come across as moodiness or disapproval.

Clearly, such an unvarying approach doesn't allow for much uncertainty. Successful relationships rely on partners being able to take turns to be the strong one, able to give and seek support from one another rather than bottling up their feelings. Pent up emotion comes out one way or another eventually, often explosively. Others will say the strong one rarely gets annoyed 'but when they do they completely blow their top'.

Hurry up

The *hurry up* driver is associated with people who are always on the go. They get things done – often ahead of schedule – but they can be very exhausting to be around. They often speak very fast, can't sit still and are always packing more into their time. They're not always realistic about how much is possible and may complain about being overworked and put upon. Nor are they always good at relaxing, so are either bored on holidays or herding everyone onto sightseeing excursions. When frustrated – such as in a traffic jam – they become irritable or angry.

Again, this driver can make it difficult to enjoy time with the family, and it's easy to see how tempers could become frayed with a partner who was more laid back. For many people, relaxing this driver would leave them with thoughts they'd prefer to avoid, introducing doubt and uncertainty.

Please others

Though often popular and kind, people using this driver can be irritating as they rarely say what they want, but may be disappointed when others don't know. Because they rely on other people to make them feel OK, they're easily hurt and let down. They often defend themselves ferociously when criticised, so can find themselves in surprisingly conflictual relationships. This is especially the case if their partner has a *be strong* driver and they need lots of reassurance. Ultimately, they may grow resentful and feel taken for granted, which just feeds the feelings of inadequacy that the *please others* driver is meant to overcome.

Try hard

People with a *try hard* driver sometimes find themselves in manipulative or outright abusive relationships because they always believe things would be better if they just made a bit more effort. As a result, they can be talked back into an unhealthy relationship by the mere suggestion that they haven't given it enough of a go – even if their partner has made no effort at all. They may need to learn that just because someone else wants them to do something, it doesn't mean they have to agree. Like the person with a *please others* driver, they don't always realise that being able to say no, and taking care of themselves, allows them to be more available to others when they're genuinely needed and more able to assess realistically what it's possible to achieve. Similarly to those with a *be strong* or *please others* driver, they may find it hard to identify and then be clear about their own needs and may not ask for help. They have only one strategy for feeling good enough, which entirely relies on others to validate their efforts. Yet again, the pursuit of certainty leads instead to insecurity and doubt.

Becoming aware of your major driver, and becoming more flexible, offers a wider range of options with which to function and makes us more open and curious about meaning. This may seem less certain, but uncertainty offers more safety as it will allow you to gather more information and thereby to make meaning more usefully. Other messages are often subsidiary versions of these main drivers, but it's still worth identifying them, as you can create other messages that make the drivers more manageable when you find them compelling. For instance, you could:

- change *be perfect* to *be yourself*
- change *be strong* to *you can have needs*
- change *hurry up* to *relax and take your time*
- change *please others* to *please yourself*
- change *try hard* to *plan and proceed.*

It can be difficult to stop using the drivers so exclusively, because the outcomes are very vague. What is perfect, for instance? How would you know if you were being strong enough? How fast should you hurry? How hard should you try? Though pleasing others would appear easy to judge, it's actually really difficult because the person with a *please others* driver often pays more attention to criticism than praise, even though they seek it. They may also find it difficult to read praise when it's offered and, even then, it's probably either never enough or they don't know how to trust it or what to do with it.

The *try hard* driver often leads people to leave tasks incomplete, as it's the trying rather than the outcome that matters to them. They can be disorganised too so, if this sounds like you, it makes sense to spend more time planning and following your directions to the end. The pleasure you'll experience from achievement may convince you to change.

Exercise: Drivers

If you have difficulty identifying your drivers, try this exercise.

1. Make a list of all the people from your childhood who may have influenced you.
2. Imagine they each had a coat of arms. What would the motto be? Write a phrase, saying or piece of advice for each person. It could be one of the drivers or something different.

3. See if any similar themes emerge, or recurring mottos.
4. Try to think of some examples of how these mottos were expressed by the person or people you've attributed them to.
5. Then think of some examples that show how they might be affecting your own life.
6. Consider how they might be influencing your relationship or how past relationships may have been affected.
7. Is there anything you would like to change or do differently?
8. What more positive drivers could you use instead?

Some of the mottos you come up with may seem more positive than the drivers, such as:

- Follow your dreams
- Be happy
- Seize the day
- Be kind
- Do your best.

When you look at the above list closely, however, they can seem very similar to the original list of drivers. Neither are a problem in themselves, as they all offer motivation and a structure for your beliefs. When they are followed slavishly, though, they close down alternatives so effectively that you may not realise any other options are available. *Be happy*, for instance, is a terribly restrictive motto, as being happy all the time denies the negative feelings we inevitably experience at least occasionally.

Sometimes we come up with mottos that aren't positive messages, but rather are injunctions *not* to do something. The following list was devised by US psychologist John McNeel (2010), because so many of his clients identified these messages as compellingly influencing them:

- Don't be (don't exist)
- Don't be who you are
- Don't be a child
- Don't grow up
- Don't succeed
- Don't do anything
- Don't be important
- Don't belong

- Don't be close
- Don't be well (don't be sane)
- Don't think
- Don't feel.

Combined with your driver, these injunctions can present a power-fully organising way of being. For example, the injunction *don't succeed* may have been conveyed alongside the driver *be perfect*, demanding an impossible way of being. The injunction *don't be separate* alongside *please others* requires that the person gives up their individuality to the service of the other person, group or family. *Don't belong* alongside *please others*, however, requires a separation or otherness that isolates the person, possibly leading them to seek approval while never feeling able to bask in it.

We all convey messages unconsciously, usually with no intention of coercing, influencing or hurting. However, circumstances and context affect what we say and how it's received. This means that, even if both you and your partner had been exposed to the same messages and drivers, you probably still wouldn't behave in the same way or develop the same meanings. Given that there are 12 basic injunctions and five drivers, there are scores of potential combinations, so finding someone with the same ones is unlikely anyway. It's more likely that you'll be attracted to someone who has challenging drivers and injunctions. So someone with a *be strong/ don't be close* combination may have a partner with *try hard/don't be important*. The strong and remote first combination might struggle with the potentially needy and insecure second combination. That's why attempting to become aware of your own combination helps to expand your repertoire of drivers and injunctions – in other words, to be less certain.

Once again, because we're not necessarily conscious of these injunctions, it's easy to assume that the way we think is shared by everyone else. Indeed, feeling part of a shared humanity or experience is something we actively seek. Think of the fervour with which we support our favourite team, respond to a heart-wrenching story in the media or collectively mourn the death of a famous personality. More ominously, factions will sometimes form to exclude someone or some group of people they consider threatening. Prejudice and oppression like this can be an outward manifestation of inner doubts; an externalised search for certainty (Morgan and Thomas, 1996). Families do this too, nominating a black sheep or problem child to carry the family insecurity. We often feel 'difficult' people nominate themselves, when actually they may have been subtly positioned in ways that encourage them to sacrifice themselves. This happens between couples too, especially when they have feelings of being not good enough, which may be consciously experienced or deeply repressed.

Psychiatrist Thomas A. Harris (2012) came up with four life positions that reflect the way people see the world and which, therefore, influence their relationships:

- I'm not OK, you're OK
- I'm not OK, you're not OK
- I'm OK, you're not OK
- I'm OK, you're OK.

The first of these, *I'm not OK, you're OK*, reflects low self-esteem and awareness of shame. Someone like this will probably put other people's needs before their own and may feel that any positive behaviour towards them will always be conditional. From this position, for instance, you may expect to be treated badly and treat others with resentful deference. You may also be afraid of criticism and afraid to criticise, even when you're badly treated.

The second position, *I'm not OK, you're not OK*, is often taken by people who have been neglected or abused. They have low self-worth, are full of shame, expect little or nothing from others and are unlikely to value relationships. *I'm OK, you're not OK* may develop in someone who is able to bypass their shame and avoid not-good-enough feelings. It can also result from having to be very self-reliant, perhaps in a busy family or one where little emotion is shown. It isn't hard to imagine this making someone less understanding or tolerant of others. They often find partners who occupy the *I'm not OK, you're OK* position.

The final *I'm OK, you're OK* position develops in people who are comfortable in themselves, aware of their not-good-enough feelings and able to manage them. Most significantly, they expect to be treated well by others. This is also an 'adult' way of being, whereas the others can seem more appropriate for critical parents or children. Coming from an unblaming, secure adult position is more likely to encourage your partner to occupy that position too.

Obviously, these positions can't be changed overnight, but you can try to be more aware of them, to notice your partner's behaviour too and to consider how this fits with your own. Just becoming aware of the way you see yourself and the world will almost certainly make you notice the way you treat others and the possibility that you're misconstruing others' intentions. Sometimes it helps to observe how other people manage uncertainty and change, as in the case of Pilar and Jill.

Pilar and Jill

Despite her senior job in retail, Pilar had very little confidence. She often felt people were laughing at her, assumed they were more capable and thought they knew more than she did. She was always apologising. When she met Jill, she was immediately struck by how open she was. She didn't seem to be ashamed of negative feelings and it was noticeable that when she made mistakes she just apologised and tried to learn from what had happened. Pilar felt she could never be like Jill and was amazed that Jill was interested in her.

As their relationship developed, Pilar became more and more certain that it was only a matter of time until Jill would see her flaws and leave her. She found herself pushing Jill away emotionally and becoming sulky and withdrawn. She didn't want to be like this but she didn't trust her feelings – or Jill. Very soon, she felt cracks were developing in the relationship, but still Jill didn't dump her. In fact, Jill carried on making plans for them both and didn't seem to have changed. Pilar assumed this meant Jill couldn't be all that interested in her or she would have been more upset by her moodiness.

One day Pilar overheard Jill telling a friend she was worried about Pilar and thought she might be depressed. Pilar was convinced this was the end, that Jill was fed up with her moods after all and thought there was something wrong with her. She wrote a letter to Jill finishing the relationship and apologising for being so hopeless. She was amazed and overwhelmed when Jill sought her out. Instead of being angry, she cried and hugged her, asking where on earth she got the idea she was hopeless. There was no miraculous overnight change in Pilar, and Jill *did* sometimes become exasperated with her lack of confidence, but they both tried harder to check what the other was feeling and meaning. Very gradually, Pilar stopped making negative assumptions and began to trust Jill, and the rest of the world too.

Becoming uncertain

Pilar's certain way of looking at the world didn't allow her to investigate or doubt, both of which are important aspects of being able to self-soothe. If we're unable to consider other points of view, we're much more likely to become upset and steam into battle needlessly. Uncertainty is an essential component of self-talk, the ability to calm ourselves down rather than catastrophise and allow negativity to escalate. If someone's upset you, for instance, and you've jumped to the conclusion that they've done this deliberately, it's extremely helpful to be able to consider alternative intentions until such time as you're able to ask calmly what you were meant to think. Unfortunately, when upset, many people feel their whole bodies and minds are flooded with pain. They can't think straight, so start blaming and lashing out unfiltered. Needless to say, this is only likely to make matters worse.

Removing yourself from an upsetting situation or person is a good idea (also discussed in Chapter 5). There may be someone you can contact to help you calm down, but it's also important to have strategies to calm yourself when there's no one there. Developing helpful self-talk is, therefore, essential. Self-talk can remind you of what you don't know, steer you away from certainty and help you to start considering alternatives to your assumptions, which may reveal that the situation isn't as bad as you thought. It may also be helpful to review your past experiences of the person or situation, as we often hope people will behave in ways that they've never done before.

Mandy and Kelvin

Mandy was disappointed every Valentine's Day because her partner Kelvin never gave her red roses, though he always splashed out on a restaurant meal with champagne. She never hinted that she would have preferred roses, so Kelvin was oblivious to her disappointment. If she'd investigated, she would have learned that Kelvin remembered a comment she'd made about hating 'cheesy' gifts, so he also avoided chocolates and soft toys. What's more, Mandy suffered from hay fever, another reason for him to exclude flowers.

Mandy had a thought and stuck with it, never questioning it, because she came from a *not OK* position and expected people to let her down. Because she was unable to consider alternatives, and allow uncertainty, her negative beliefs about herself were reinforced. To her, Kelvin's failure to buy her roses meant he didn't love her. She was focused on not getting what she wanted and what that meant to her, rather than being able to appreciate the bigger picture, which was much more reassuring. She also never considered the possibility that she could ask Kelvin to buy her roses. In her mind, he should just know what she wanted. Of course, if she'd really stopped to think about this she would have realised he couldn't know.

She didn't feel deserving but she still hoped she was, and pinned her hopes on random 'evidence', such as being bought roses, which just served to let her down over and over again. If she'd been less certain, more curious and more able to take responsibility for her own feelings – rather than relying on Kelvin's non-existent mind-reading abilities – she would have had real evidence that he cared for her and wanted to please her.

Mentoring

If you think like Mandy, developing effective self-talk is particularly hard, as you're probably more used to creating a story about how you want a situation to play out. As an alternative, imagining what advice you'd give to a best friend in your situation is a good start. Another is to cultivate an imaginary mentor who can help guide you through difficulties. To make this effective, it's helpful to iden-tify what qualities your mentor needs. For instance, if you would like to be calmer and to be better at letting go of arguments, you'd want a mentor who'd be good at that. You can choose anyone – a real person, celebrity, historical figure or fictional character. Family members are not such good choices, as they're likely to share some of your own unhelpful thinking.

The point is to be able to imagine asking the mentor for advice and to follow what they offer. So, when you walk away from a row and are desperate to go back and tell your partner just what you think of them, your mentor will be able to distract you, explain why going back isn't a good idea, reassure you that it'll be better tomorrow – or whatever else it is you need to get you through. Another good idea is to write yourself a message, or record one on your phone, for the moments that you find the most difficult. The message needs to be affirmative and soothing, something you know you'd want to hear in times of trouble. Some people carry their messages with them so they can consult them at any time. A message for Mandy might say: 'You're a good person and you need to take care of yourself, so walk away from this row and take the time you need to calm down.'

Managing stress

The aim of all this is for you to be able to look after yourself so you can enjoy your life when you're alone and not feel that other people – and particularly your partner – have the only key to your wellbeing. Managing stress and tension in your everyday life can help with this. One way is to identify many points during the day when you have something to look forward to. For instance, anticipating breakfast and a hot shower might be what gets you out of bed. Then you might be looking forward to listening to music, the news or a podcast on the way to work. While you travel, you'll be thinking of the cup of coffee you'll have when you arrive. Taking the attitude that the day is full of pleasures – maybe a breath of fresh air, chats with colleagues, a tasty lunch – can help to keep you going from one task to the next. It's great to have a few treats in the diary too, not just outings and entertainment but family or couple time and even time for sex. Weekends away and holidays spread throughout the year, if you can afford them, also give you something to be excited about.

Looking forward with pleasure and excitement releases healthy endorphins which increase feelings of wellbeing and positivity. Other endorphin activators include exercise, feelings of achievement and enjoyment itself. So being in the moment and really appreciating those things you look forward to can bring even more pleasure and satisfaction, as can remembering them afterwards.

Exercise: Activity scoring

A way of increasing your sense of achievement is to score all your activities out of ten for pleasure and usefulness. Choose a different hour each day to score every single thing you do – say, 7am–8am on day 1, 8am–9am on day 2 and so on. For instance, you might start the day by lying in bed thinking about getting up, so you'd score yourself low for usefulness but high for pleasure as you start the day by enjoying the warmth and comfort of your bed. Getting out of bed may score high for usefulness and low for pleasure. However, eating breakfast and washing may receive high scores for both.

This process encourages you to think more positively about your life. Scoring and reviewing your scores requires mindful focus, and even allows you to consider what might be more pleasant or useful. For instance, taking your lunch to the park may give you some useful exercise and be more pleasant than buying a sandwich and eating it as you walk back to your desk.

Not only does this sort of mindful appreciation and anticipation flood your body with comforting hormones, but it also acknowledges that you expect and deserve pleasure and satisfaction. This is an important step in developing self-care and self-validation. Limiting use of social media, rather than checking every ping, also gives you something to anticipate and look forward to. However, if you've been relying on other people to make you feel good about yourself, it may be helpful to avoid posts that you hope will generate lots of responses. Although this can give you a boost, it can also lower your mood and encourage obsessional checking.

Keeping 'to do' lists offers the satisfaction of ticking jobs off as they're completed, but lists of what you've done can also offer considerable satisfaction as you watch them grow. The 'bittiest' days, when we've been busy with small tasks, can leave us feeling little sense of accomplishment. However, these are often the most productive, and listing what you do as you complete each task demonstrates this.

Asking for help

Many people's focus is on what they don't like rather than what they do enjoy, and particularly on the lack of support they feel they deserve. You could improve feelings of wellbeing by asking (taking control) rather than hoping (and being disappointed). Avoiding asking for help takes a great deal more energy and effort than learning to ask for help when you need it. If you find this difficult, you could set up small asking experiments – for a cup of tea, to pass the pepper, to put something away.

Some people think they ask, but what they actually do is nag when they don't get what they want. Being polite, clear and consistent about your expectations, and showing your appreciation, does get results. If others see your requests as demands, on the other hand, they'll resist. Dealing with the negative cycles that develop from this sort of issue is the subject of Chapter 9.

Remember: Embracing uncertainty allows us to be more curious about others' motivation and behaviour, increasing our ability to self-soothe rather than expecting others to regulate our feelings.

Bibliography

Harris, T. A. (2012) *I'm OK, You're OK*, London: Arrow.

Kahler, T. (1975) Drivers – the key to the process script, *Transactional Analysis Journal*, 5(3), 280–284.

Lewandowski, G. W., Mattingly, B. A. and Pedreiro, A. (2014) Under pressure: The effects of stress on positive and negative relationship behaviours. *The Journal of Social Psychology*, 154, 463–473.

McNeel, J. R. (2010) Understanding the power of injunctive messages and how they are resolved in redecision therapy. *Transactional Analysis Journal*, 40(2), 159–169.

Morgan, H. and Thomas, K. (1996) A psychodynamic perspective on group processes. In M. Wetherell (ed.) *Identities, Groups and Social Issues*, London: Sage.

Rodriguez, A. J. and Margolin, G. (2013) Wives' and husbands' cortisol reactivity to proximal and distal dimensions of family conflict. *Family Process*, 52, 555–569.

Symoens, S. and Bracke, P. (2015) Work-family conflict and mental health and recently cohabiting couples: A couple perspective. *Health Sociology Review*, 24(1), 48–63.

Chapter 9

Breaking and avoiding negative cycles

Repeated unhelpful behaviour patterns develop when couples try to have their needs met indirectly, rather than being clear about what they want. Even in second and subsequent relationships, couples can be surprisingly reluctant to negotiate boundaries and rules, even ones concerning issues that have the potential to compromise trust. Reluctance to rock the boat and appear to be introducing a problem when all is currently fine may be behind this. However, life changes us, as our experiences affect our expectations and areas of sensitivity. We develop comfort zones, both in relation to the physical world and our thinking. From what we eat for breakfast to how to vote, our beliefs and personal rules need consideration. Given that our comforts and ideals were unlikely to have been anywhere near as developed when we embarked on our early romantic relationships, they'll probably have changed quite a bit since the first time we fell in love. The initial task, then, is to recognise what might cause trouble.

Though your partner may find them baffling, it's natural to have sensitivities to certain behaviours, especially any that caused distress in previous relationships. For instance, your partner may do no more than suggest some minor change in your home, but to you it feels as if they're taking over or criticising. Even if you feel you're being unreasonable, it's important that you don't just go along with behaviours or wishes that spark negative feelings for you. Unaddressed, this could threaten the relationship by causing anxiety and resentment. When it's entirely possible to explain your feelings and negotiate, don't stay quiet. Bear in mind that it can be the minor acts of thoughtlessness that create the most distress and lead to arguments. This is even more likely if your partner has no idea you're not happy with something.

Many, if not most, couples move in together without ever having a discussion about how this will work. You may have no idea, say, that your partner always watches the six o'clock news with their dinner on their lap and their feet soaking in a bowl of mustardy hot water. Even if neither of you has such outlandish routines, you *will* certainly have habits and preferences and it's a good idea to think about how you'll accommodate them. Being honest about potential areas of sensitivity makes it less likely that either of you will jump to conclusions. If, for example, your ex had a problem with money or drinking, these are areas where you'll probably be keeping an eye out. There are less obvious cues where you might find yourself reacting to the way you're spoken to or something that's implied, and both you and your partner are taken aback by the strength of your response.

Of course, your partner will have acquired sensitivities too, which *you'll* need to understand. Failure to address possible differences in approach creates potential landmines, lurking beneath the surface, ready to explode when approached. Only addressing them in arguments makes them even hotter topics, to be avoided. Issues come up naturally, but many of us are good at changing the subject if we sense disagreement. If so, you may need to consciously bring up some of the concerns, especially if you really don't have a clue what your partner thinks. The topics for discussion listed in Chapter 4 (pages 54–57) cover many of the issues you may wish to tackle. This doesn't need to be gloom-laden. An upbeat approach to such conversations, which sees them as exciting ways to plan and anticipate your future together, will encourage positivity even when sensitive issues are discussed.

Being respectful

Many relationship difficulties are just down to misunderstanding, and no offence was ever intended. The problem is that, once we feel unheard, bullied or disrespected, we become even more attuned to examples of what we don't like and also put up defences. Even the most fiercely argumentative couple can become loving and appreciative once they begin to understand each other's motivation. When they become more curious about each other, rather than just making negative assumptions, the meaning they make of each other's behaviour changes completely.

The way we speak to each other positions us, and we position ourselves in relation to others. Some people think that being in a close relationship means that anything they say or do should be acceptable, and they're offhand and disrespectful towards their partner. Similarly, coming from a family that enjoys a great deal of banter leads to teasing. To the partner from a more circumspect family, this may feel like bullying. They have no way of knowing that what they're experiencing isn't meant personally. If they lack confidence, or fear causing offence, they're never likely to see banter as a complement to closeness. It will always seem like an insult or, worse, an exercise of power.

In a nutshell, don't assume that behaviours that come naturally to you are also comfortable to others. This is even more important when a partner is known to have been in a particularly unbalanced or abusive relationship in the past. How power is expressed may not just determine whether it succeeds, but also how willing or able you both become to engage in any relationship in future.

Using power

So-called 'power struggles' between partners often stem from feelings of unfairness or not being heard, which may have originated in relationships with family, teachers or other people of influence in our lives, including previous partners. How we've been treated in the past creates our expectation of how we'll be treated now. If you have little experience of successful negotiation in your family and earlier relationships, you may try to meet needs through manipulation, omission or deceit.

Strategies to avoid arguments are examples of collaborative conversations which use *power-with* each other rather than *power-over*. The psychotherapist Mona Fishbane (2011) urges couples to distinguish between *power-over* and *power-to*. *Power-over* is the exercise of control, whereas *power-to* is the ability to make changes. Confusing these when they feel helpless can lead partners to use *power-over* the other. This is likely to interfere with development of *power-to* behaviours, especially if it pushes the other person to be unco-operative or makes them feel helpless. This means one partner has all the responsibility as well as all the control, while the other partner may feel unable to do anything.

This kind of dynamic can develop when one partner has been expected to take unrealistic practical or emotional responsibility for others, particularly close adults, when they were growing up. It consequently comes naturally to them to assume control, but they often then become bitter at 'having to do everything'. This can lead to the kind of endless nagging that leaves each partner raw and resentful. When the 'controlled' partner does what's required, they often find themselves in trouble for not doing it properly.

The controlling partner may be driven by the need to make everything perfect. This can happen particularly if they've had parents who blamed and criticised them or even just implied that they could do better or that they were disappointed. They're likely to be following a script that promises dire consequences if perfection isn't achieved (see also pages 52 and 54). If they ever stopped to think this through, they'd realise they create their own consequences. Controlling themselves and everything else may have been important to avoid punishment as a child – but that time is over and their need to control has become inappropriate. In this case, the person who's controlling is likely to be someone who needs appreciation and affirmation that they're doing OK. However, many partners respond by withdrawing and going along with whatever seems to be required – 'anything for a quiet life'.

If this is you, what might work better would be to show your partner the appreciation they crave. Commenting positively may take a bit of getting used to for both of you, so you may be snapped at to begin with, but persistence should pay off. Give it a couple of weeks and you'll almost certainly find your partner softens, appreciates you more and you'll both start to move closer to a collaborative *power-with* way of being together. Another way of changing your dynamic could be to ask for guidance. If you expect to be criticised for whatever you do, ask if how you've done it is all right. Own up to things you find difficult. Tell your partner calmly if the way they speak to you is upsetting or makes you think there's no point in trying. If this is a new relationship, explain that this is not the way you feel partners should be.

Creating change

To achieve any change in a relationship, you have to be able to get outside your own head. As Chapter 8 made clear, it can be a massive problem for your relationship if you habitually play out scenarios in your imagination and believe what happens in them, rather than what's really going on in the outside world. Not only can this lead to becoming aggrieved with a partner who hasn't actually done what you've been fantasising, but it can lead you to expect behaviours that your partner doesn't know are required. Lorraine, for instance, imagined Greg proposing to her in a dreamy setting. So she set up a romantic evening, which they both thoroughly enjoyed, but when the night ended without a proposal Lorraine went into a sulk. Greg had no idea what was wrong, especially as the behaviour was entirely out of keeping with the great time they'd just had.

It's fruitless to believe that your partner can guess what you're thinking, ought to be able to if they cared enough or could know if they bothered to try. It's also crucial not to assume that *you* know what your partner is thinking. Indeed, the best way to begin to change a difficult or conflictual relationship is often to become curious, to start wondering whether you're correct about your partner's reasons for thinking and behaving the way they do. You may assume they want to hurt you, but it's more likely they're just doing what they always do, which means protecting themselves from what they see as yet another critical or attacking person – this time, that's *you*. Be honest with yourself and ask whether you ever really listen to what your partner's saying or do you just hammer home your own argument? Often, repeated arguments lose their currency even though they may have some merit, and there may be good reasons why they don't go away. Buried or obvious, arguments are about unmet needs that will never be met if rowing doesn't stop.

It's more likely that jealousy and resentment exist where partners aren't able to state their needs but, equally, are unable to manage their own feelings. Couples who respond to gut feelings and fears, rather than what's been discussed or is happening, are more likely to pay attention to what they imagine their partner will do or think. When at least one partner can manage their own feelings, both the relationship and each person are able to develop too. These partners learn to trust that they and the relationship can find strategies to cope with difficulty and are less worried by unpredictability. When they're less good at self-management, the relationship feels less secure, and the couple are more likely to be motivated by a need for reassurance than by interest and care. This is why curiosity, interest and avoidance of assumptions are necessary from the very start.

How you communicate

It's difficult not to be affected by your partner's behaviour, but if you're powerfully drawn to them and want to be together it's worth recognising the control you have by not allowing yourself to be triggered. If you're busy concentrating on being interested and curious, this is much easier. Just acknowledging difference can *make* a difference; developing curiosity about your differences can be very rewarding. For example, some partners bend over backwards not to show their feelings, while others think that self-disclosure is the same as interest and love. Could this characterise your relationship? One partner may feel battered by the barrage of feelings and needs constantly being expressed, while the other may feel the relationship is barren and that they're doing all the work.

A problem can be that thoughts are randomly tossed out with little structure or signposting about what's expected or needed. You might think that issues can just be discussed as you go, part of everyday conversation and no big deal. However, this can leave both sides confused and dissatisfied. Before tackling an important issue, ask yourself the following:

- What's the most important point to get across about this issue?
- What do I want to change?
- What do I think the outcome will be?
- How realistic is this?

It's also worth asking yourself whether there's any evidence for the concerns or anxieties you're experiencing. If not, think about what's making you anxious. For instance, let's say that your new partner is staying with you every night and you're finding this intrusive. However, you fear that, if you ask them to go home, they'll end the relationship. Thinking about why you have this anxiety, you realise that your fear could stem from your previous relationship in which your partner always threatened to leave when you wanted something different from them. There may be no evidence that your new partner will do that.

What you want to convey:

- You love having your partner stay over, but it feels almost as if you're living together and it's too early in the relationship for that.
- You need some time to clean the house, go shopping, do some paid work and see your friends and family.

The outcome you want:

• You'd like them to stay over two or three nights a week at the most for the time being, and to maintain contact via phone, text and social media on the other days.

A conversation like this could be conducted fairly quickly. Unfortunately, many of us go all round the houses or try to set up situations where the other person does what we want without us having to ask. Consequently, unwanted situations keep on recurring. In the above example, the other partner would almost certainly agree to the request, though they may try to negotiate a bit or offer to help with cleaning. Only if they were very insecure would they take what you say as a brush-off. Even so, it's not your responsibility that they feel disappointed. We all need to take charge of our own feelings. Indeed, it could be seen as highly manipulative of them to prevent you from stating your wishes because you're afraid of their reaction.

Happy Hour

Busy millennials have learned to timetable important conversations. A weekly Happy Hour can be used for each partner to bring up something they need to discuss, ideally at a regular time which is free of distractions. The hour is split into three sections in which each partner has 20 minutes for their topic, while the final third is used to synchronise diaries.

During your 20 minutes, the headlines of your point should be briefly outlined, followed by the outcome you're looking for, as above. This is then negotiated for the remainder of the 20 minutes, after which most people start repeating themselves. It's important to decide how this will work. For instance, if you don't agree with what's being suggested, you need to give a reason or at least promise to think it over. The idea is to use negotiation and compromise, not to bulldoze your ideas onto the other partner or to just accept whatever's proposed even if it doesn't work for you. Similarly, it's really cheating to filibuster for 20 minutes and hope the conversation will go away.

If you don't think you can have any sort of conversation without arguing, try writing down what you want. Some couples communicate by text or e-mail, which at least gives a record of what's being asked. However, the request or point of the message is often lost in amongst rambling accusations and criticisms.

An I Want–I Will Book (Campbell, 2015) can overcome this if you both agree to stick to a single sentence request or response. The idea is that you have an exercise book with *I Want* written at the head of a left-hand page and *I Will* written at the head of the opposite page. So one partner might write, 'I want you to kiss me goodbye when you leave the house' and the other might reply, 'I will try to remember to do that' or 'I will try, but you may have to remind me!' This only works if both partners agree to check every day whether the book has been updated and to use it only for requests and responses, rather than criticism.

Many couples' lives have been transformed by this, because they don't object to one another's messages. What hurts and provokes them is the way they speak to each other, so much so that even when one becomes more measured the other doesn't notice.

Managing media

Conflict is likely to happen more quickly and ferociously if you've had troubled relationships before. It can become almost second nature to be in competition or dispute with your partner. Indeed, even as recently as the 1990s, the media and comedians were still making a living out of jokes depicting how couples outwit each other, employing stereotypes of battle-axe women and sex-crazed, duplicitous men. This sort of gender pigeonholing was so pervasive that dishonest and conflictual relationships became normalised. Though we've moved on a bit, there are still many people around who were exposed to this way of thinking for decades and who expect competition and conflict rather than affection and appreciation, even though this may be what they long for. What's more, the internet and social media has provided a new source of influence to make us feel we're not doing our relationship properly or that it doesn't look good enough in the eyes of the world. So, instead of just feeling it's hard to sustain the relationship we're living, we have to live up to its image, splattered all over the web. Because other people may post images or messages that tag or include us, the way we're portrayed can easily feel out of control.

Self-image is inevitably affected by those around us, the way we're treated and the way we think others see us. Now an added complication is that you or other people may object to what some-one else has posted from an occasion when you were present. This is leading to more partner disputes, which often seem petty and unfair. It has to be remembered that we all rebuild our image post-relationship, and what we're striving for can seem to be destroyed in an instant by a thoughtless post, particularly when it's then misinterpreted. Online communication and social media has also become a battleground and a source of information for partners who feel compelled to stalk each other online. This often leads to out-of-the-blue accusations, sulks or revenge behaviour which the person may just feel is a reflection of their insecurity but which, objectively, amounts to abuse. Some people even go to lengths that involve breaking the law.

How we treat each other's phones, e-mail and social media sites should be one of the first areas where boundaries are agreed. It's common for a partner to say there should be no need for privacy in a relationship where partners trust each other and there is nothing to hide. However, equally, in trusting relationships there should be no need to demand access to pin numbers or to try to catch your partner out. Denying one another privacy *is* abusive, so don't be tempted to compromise on this for a quiet life or because not to do so would threaten the relationship. This just proves the relationship is already under threat.

People often resort to surveillance behaviour because they've been hurt in the past and want to control their partner in order to prevent future pain. What actually happens is that they create their own suspicion and panic, damaging the relationship in the process and often contributing to the situation they fear. Usually, such part-ners think all would be well if they could change the other – this way of thinking isn't just futile, it's downright daft. If we want change, we need to start with ourselves, where we do have control. The smallest change in one partner is likely to make a difference to the other. This doesn't mean bending over backwards to please an abusive partner who'll never be satisfied; it does mean adopt-ing healthy approaches to self-care and communication. After all, it takes two to make a battle, and you can choose not to fight.

In your new relationship, you may find yourself needing to expli-citly negotiate what you both see as reasonable use of technology. If it seems intrusive, it may help to ring-fence times when tech-nology isn't used – mealtimes and dates are an obvious example. Spillover of work into home life and leisure time – also discussed in

Chapter 8 – is inevitable as we're all so easily contactable, and it's particularly tempting to keep checking e-mail if work is stressful or exciting. This can, however, leave you with no space for yourself, your relationship or family, thereby increasing your stress.

Some couples ban phones in the bedroom, as their use during the night disturbs the other partner and is distracting during lovemaking. Some people start the day by looking at their phone or tablet while still in bed, which the other partner may resent, particularly if *they* like to start the day with a chat or a cuddle. Clearly, looking at your device rather than your partner while having a conversation can be construed as rude or rejecting. If your partner can't resist constantly looking at a device, there is even more reason to time-table technology-free times to talk.

It may also be important to agree how much you contact each other during the day. You'll both be frustrated if you're expecting a response to all your messages when your partner is too busy to respond. It's helpful to be able to contact one another, but do agree what's acceptable or even possible so that neither of you is disappointed. Do also agree what sort of messages are OK. Some people write incredibly long, rambling e-mails and even texts which leave a record of complaints, criticism and nagging long after the complained-about event is forgotten.

Nagging

If you find yourself accused of nagging or become aware that you blame or criticise, ask yourself whether you'd really be happy if your partner got things right, even if you feel resentful about having to do everything yourself. Is there some satisfaction in blaming? Really think hard about whether working together might make life easier. You'd have to give up the blaming and learn to compromise, but instead you might discover what it's like to feel supported. At some level, many people fear that becoming too close will leave them vulnerable – blaming and bickering are ways to maintain emotional distance and self-protection. But they make life miserable. Accepting that perfection isn't possible, and its pursuit is pointless, gives you the option to be more open, close and calm rather than being controlled by a futile need to get everything right. In the end, there are no prizes anyway.

Meanwhile, there are benefits to be gained from finding out what your partner wants, rather than making assumptions and avoiding their needs. When your partner speaks to you, what they'll be looking for is one of three things: comfort/support, guidance, or to chill out with you (Hill et al., 2014). Relationship conflict results when what you both want or need is misread. For instance, partners often each believe that the other only wants to blame them. No other motivation occurs to either of them, so their defences are up and they both engage in blaming.

Think for a moment what underlies accusations. They're often used when someone doesn't feel good enough and they want to shift their not-good-enough feelings away from themselves. So what they really want is to be comforted and made to feel good enough, to be able to believe they're OK. Understanding this may help you not to be triggered by a blaming partner and to offer the care and concern they crave, rather than blaming and criticising as well. However, though becoming a blaming and angry partner is likely to result from years of being misunderstood, criticised and not having needs met, it's not an excuse to reproduce your bad experience. Inflicting this on others just invites more misunderstanding, blame and rejection to be levelled at you. You'll actually feel more on top of things if you take a step back.

It's really difficult to escape from patterns of negativity, so relationship counselling may be needed to accelerate what may seem an impossible process. However, you can experiment with changes to your own behaviour to see whether you feel better and more in control. After all, every time you repeat the same old cycle, you're effectively letting it control you. A good start is to give more consideration to which battles need fighting. Think through the consequences of commenting on, say, whether the marmalade was put back in the right place and why it matters. If you're able to talk calmly with your partner about the way you treat each other, you could use the exercise below to see if there's a way to break out of damaging dynamics.

Exercise: Talking point

- Discuss what happens between you. How do arguments or blaming begin? Can you spot any triggers? How do each of you feel at the time? What motivates you to blame?
- If the blaming or arguing process, or the feelings you have at the time, could come alive, what would this look like? Would they take the form of a live creature, like a monster, something inanimate like a stone, something weather-related like a cloud,

wind or huge wave? Sometimes the dynamic can be seen as a
hole you fall into or a cloak that envelops you both.

• Describe this to each other and what it feels like when it
  becomes active.
• What qualities do you need to overcome it? How could you
  help each other to reduce its powers?

Some couples sidestep the need to adapt to each other by assuming differences are insurmountable – but that doesn't necessarily
stop them from trying to change each other. So one of the reasons
this exercise can be helpful is that it shows how you each experience the same process differently. You may have similar ideas or
describe something completely different, but the point is to be
able to talk together about what this feeling and behaviour is like
for you. One may see the arguing pattern as being like a cloak of
despair while the other imagines a huge boulder rolling towards
them. If you can each recognise and describe this, listen and tolerate the differences in your descriptions, you'll have taken a giant
step towards dealing together with the subjects you argue about.
The management of uncertainty, discussed in Chapter 8, will ena-
ble you to avoid unnecessary conflict. Ultimately, you may be able
to jointly imagine some sort of entity that you can fight together.
Until then, it helps to be aware of the monster/black cloud/cold
wind affecting each of you. You may start being able to avoid its
effects sometimes, as you both become more determined not to
let it win.

Cultural differences

Couples whose cultural differences are more obvious, such as those
brought up in different countries or different areas of a country,
with different religions, from different social classes or educational
backgrounds, know they have to learn about each other. Where
there is apparent similarity, it can be more difficult even to recognise that differences exist. Seemingly similar couples often never
have clarifying conversations, and encounter difficulties because
they wrongly assume they share the same views. This can lead to
clashes about major and minor issues, such as how often to visit
family, when they should be invited to stay, how to spend leisure
time, how much space they each need, how to dress for work, what
work to do and how to prioritise it – and on and on...

Where there are obvious cultural differences, couples are much more likely to explore and negotiate which aspects of them they will 'live' together and which aspects remain separate. Research into this has found that couples fare better when they respect each other's beliefs and recognise when it's important to make space for them, even when their day-to-day lives are lived more to one partner's cultural values than the other (Seshadri and Knudson-Martin, 2013).

Autistic spectrum

Sometimes there are mental health issues or one partner has high-functioning autistic spectrum disorder (also known as Asperger syndrome). Partners on the autistic spectrum often begin their relationship showing high levels of interest and commitment, but lose much of this when a different passion takes over. The passion may be something that you both want, such as buying a house or moving in together, planning your wedding or having a baby, but they become so involved that you feel excluded. Alternatively, the passion that excludes you may be work, a hobby or interest, a child or grandchild, friend or problem. The point is that you won't feel part of this, which can be hugely painful if you've previously been the centre of their world. The person may also frustrate you by having difficulty in prioritising, speaking bluntly without apparently thinking, putting their own needs first, having difficulty in following your explanations or instructions and being upset by crowds, social functions or various kinds of sensory input. Whether or not your partner actually has a diagnosis, but behaves in this way, it can be helpful to realise that you're not alone (see www.different-together.co.uk for information and support).

Finding sources of support and developing ways of coping that don't rely on your partner always having to make you feel better are especially important for those moments when you do need to take care of yourselves separately. This empowers you to walk away from an argument and allow the situation to calm down; it enables you to be able to see other points of view; it means your sense of self won't be damaged if you and your partner disagree. This is not to say you should become an island or that you shouldn't expect your partner to offer you comfort or support sometimes. It just means not relying on your partner for everything and taking responsibility for your own feelings and behaviour. Not doing so can even create trauma when the relationship comes under pressure, as Chapter 10 explains.

Remember: Curiosity about one another's differences helps relationships to flourish while criticism of difference encourages conflict.

Bibliography

Campbell, C. (2015) *Relate Guide to Sex & Intimacy*, London: Vermilion.

Fishbane, M. D. (2011) Facilitating relational empowerment in couple therapy. *Family Process*, 50(3), 337–352.

Hill, J., Wren, B., Alderton, J., Burck, C., Kennedy, E., Senior, R. and Broyden, N. (2014) The application of a domains-based analysis to family processes: Implications for assessment and therapy. *Journal of Family Therapy*, 36, 62–80.

Seshadri, G. and Knudson-Martin, C. (2013) How couples manage interracial and intercultural differences: Implications for clinical practice. *Journal of Marital & Family Therapy*, 39(1), 43–58.

Chapter 10

Relationship trauma

Relationships have to withstand considerable pressure, and the way each partner copes affects the other. Pain and upset often result when needs aren't met or when one partner's way of coping hurts the other. Affairs, managing the past, illness and loss are among the issues that contribute to what may be felt as deep disappointment and grief about what was not as it seemed, what is no longer possible, or what may even cause lasting trauma. Recovery from trauma may be protracted and difficult, evoking earlier attachment injuries, so the pain of a betrayal can be severe and unpredictable.

It isn't just that external events stress relationships. We each bring both our own emotional baggage to our relationships and also our own unique expectations and reactions, which partners may not understand. Not coping well when your partner is upset can be enough to break some relationships, for instance.

However, as previous chapters have emphasised, the more unable you are to manage your own feelings, the more likely it is that you'll be hurt. Some people are always on the look-out for slights and disappointment. Some expect them so much that they can't help finding them, or even making them happen. The more you hope your new relationship will be different, the more disappointed you'll be if it has echoes of the past. This is less likely if you're proactive about taking control and negotiating how you want the relationship to be, rather than just waiting to see how it turns out. This doesn't mean complaining and blaming when it doesn't go your way. It does mean listening to each other and finding out what you each want and need, as well as identifying any sensitivities that may act as trauma triggers. These are usually related to past events that have caused distress and hurt.

Abuse

Nonetheless, some people use their partner's vulnerability to score points or inflict hurt. This is abusive. If you feel your partner is twisting what you say or do to their own advantage, is not listening to you or taking your needs into consideration, and always privileges their own wishes over yours, you should think very seriously about whether this is a relationship you want to continue. It isn't just physical violence that can cause long-term damage – abuse can also be emotional, sexual or financial. People stay with abusive partners for a variety of reasons, which include:

- it being too dangerous to leave;
- shame about not having a relationship;
- wishing to prove they're right that a relationship is OK even when others have warned them that it's not;
- not recognising, or underestimating, the significance of emotional, sexual or financial control;
- assuming responsibility for a partner's behaviour;
- a desperate need to have any sort of relationship, regardless of its quality.

Low self-esteem and feeling unworthy makes people especially vulnerable to abuse, particularly if they already have a trail of 'failed' relationships behind them. They may even believe they cause the abuse and that their partner would behave better if they just tried harder. Indeed, this is the way people are sucked back into awful relationships. Abusers can be very sorry after an incident that threatens the relationship, often asking the abused partner for help or pleading with them to try again. When the partner is once again hooked, they then revert to their old behaviours. If you come from a family where trying hard was highly valued, or where extremely high standards were expected, you may be more susceptible to this sort of appeal, as it's already part of your psychological makeup.

The use of power in relationships was mentioned in the previous chapter in terms of relational balance which, when tipped too far in favour of one partner, can become abusive. However, it can be hard to believe or accept what's happening. Coercive control is now an offence, so you shouldn't feel that no one will understand or believe what's been happening to you, however much your abusive partner insists this is the case. If you find yourself changing your behaviour to avoid a partner's anger or 'walking on eggshells', the relationship is probably abusive. Being genuinely frightened of a partner's reactions is a sign that the relationship is unequal. Nevertheless, ending the relationship may cause much distress. Sometimes people don't realise how abusive their relationship was until afterwards. Use the list below to see if a previous or current relationship contains any elements of abuse.

- **Gaslighting** is a classic abusive behaviour where your partner denies conduct or events that you believe to be true, eventually making you feel as though you're going mad.
- **Abnormal behaviour** may also be presented as normal, with you treated as the odd one for objecting.
- **Online stalking.** Your partner checks your phone, social media, messaging apps and e-mail or insists on knowing your passwords.
- **Isolation.** Your partner doesn't like your family and friends and, one way or another, limits how much contact you have with them, often persuading you to drop them.
- **Threats, intimidation and control.** If your partner makes clear there will be consequences if you don't do what they want, they're being abusive.
- **Threats of harm to themselves or others.** Abusive partners often threaten to harm themselves if you leave or don't conform. They may threaten or actually harm you, children, pets, family or friends too. The harm may be physical but is more often emotional, including turning others against you.
- **Threats to tell** others your secrets or personal information.
- **Damage to property** often takes the form of breaking items you love or which have special sentimental value.
- **Criticising, name-calling or putting you down.** Whether this only happens in private or in front of other people, it's not what should happen in a loving relationship.
- **Financial control** comes in many forms, from actually taking your money, running up debts they insist you pay or keeping you short of money for the household, to keeping you constantly pregnant, or being unavailable to help with childcare so that you can't work.

- **Criminal or unethical behaviour** is sometimes demanded, with the partner insisting that you would do what they want if you really loved them. If they really loved you, they wouldn't ask.
- **Entitlement** is common – only your partner's needs are important. If you don't do what they want, they say you're selfish, but if *you* want or need something, you're also called selfish. Sexual entitlement is common too – if you don't want sex or to be touched, it's not OK for someone else to just help themselves.

An additional feature of abuse is that you won't feel you can have an open conversation about any of these behaviours. What's more, you'll probably be aware that extricating yourself from the relationship may be easier said than done. Even if it's never happened before, the risk of actual physical violence being used increases significantly the moment you mention separation. You may consequently need a plan to leave, and to have a safe place for important belongings like money, bankcards and passport. However embarrassed you may feel, make sure your friends and family know what you're going through and seek support and advice from organisations like Women's Aid (www.womensaid. org or call 24-hour Freephone: 0808 2000 247) and Relate (www. relate.org.uk).

Infidelity

Affairs or online relationships are sometimes used in an abusive way to demean or exert control. Sometimes, too, people with abusive partners are drawn to other relationships for comfort, though these relationships may also turn out to be abusive. However, there are probably as many reasons for affairs as there are couples (also discussed in Chapter 1, page 18). Now that texting, sexting and online relationships have added an additional possibility for 'infidelity', even more couples find themselves in situations they may never have imagined possible. Again, social media and the internet can be exacerbating factors in modern relationship trauma. Many instances of what is perceived as infidelity are, for instance, conducted via e-mail, text or social media. They are, consequently, highly vulnerable to discovery or misunderstanding. In newer relationships, profound distress is often caused when one partner discovers the other hasn't removed their profile from a dating website, for instance.

Someone who has been brightening their day with, say, texts to a work colleague may be shocked to find that what seemed like no more than mild flirtation has been construed as an affair by their partner. These days, more than ever, couples need to be clear about what's acceptable. Whether it's been sexual, emotional or online, a relationship that upsets or threatens your partner requires a thorough renegotiation of boundaries and an overhaul of the ways you 'do' your life together, taking into account both sets of needs and sensitivities.

The hurt and bafflement that accompanies awareness that your apparently exclusive relationship has been breached can't be overestimated, particularly if an affair ended your last relationship. Fears about being let down in this way can take over your thinking, becoming obsessive and ruining the relationship even long after the threat has passed. A need for retribution may be very powerful, but it won't change what happened or help to repair the damage.

Focusing on what's already happened doesn't futureproof the relationship; if anything, it's likely to become more fragile. You don't need to know all the gory details of the affair, but you may desperately need to be assured that it's unlikely to happen again. However much you're reassured, though, it may be difficult to restore trust. Sadly, sometimes, there's no going back, even when the person who had the affair is truly sorry and baffled by what they've done. The hurt may be just too immense to get over, and efforts to repair the relationship only cause more pain. Occasionally, however, a tremendously hurt partner will turn a blind eye to affairs, even though they hate them, as enduring the pain seems better than losing a partner altogether.

Very often, though, couples see an affair as a wake-up call and an opportunity to reassess and spring-clean their relationship. Given the pressures of modern life and the complexities of modern relationships, it isn't surprising that partners sometimes escape into the light relief of a relationship that seems free from the baggage of home life. Often such relationships begin as mutually supportive friendships that offer the chance to unburden, but which escalate into a more unruly situation.

Once the shock of discovery has been absorbed, work needs to begin on determining how you want your relationship to be in future. Couples often say they want the relationship to go back to the way it was before, but this was the way that led to the affair. They also want to be able to completely trust each other, a state which possibly led them to take each other for granted and stop working at the relationship. Unfortunately, longing for calm can mean couples just agree to get back to some sort of normal without addressing the issues that led to problems in the first place. The serious hurt that's been caused may now be the elephant in the room.

There's a middle ground which acknowledges the pain but allows you to enjoy the relationship again. Recognising that it's not a good idea to make any rash decisions for several months, you need to be able to co-exist in a way which acknowledges the hurt but allows space to see what develops. Ideally, see if you can give yourselves a break from the high emotion you've been experiencing and try behaving as though the relationship is OK. If some ground-rules are agreed, and this period is treated as experimental, you may both find out whether it feels comfortable to be together in a loving relationship or whether this has now become impossible. Some couples feel it's too soon after a few weeks or months to try this, but the alternative is to continue a standoff indefinitely. This is exhausting and demands you each take defensive positions, which may do even more harm. If you can agree to behave *as if* all is well, while acknowledging that this doesn't mean all is forgiven or that the hurt has gone, you'll give yourselves space to think more clearly and engage in calmer discussions. Eventually, you'll be able to plan together what's possible for the future – many couples emerge happier and closer than ever.

Attachment injury

A sense of loss doesn't just apply to affairs. Any painful event can cause relationship problems for many years if it remains unresolved. For instance, Helga felt Max was unsupportive when she had a miscarriage. Though Max has always argued that he didn't know what more Helga expected from him, Helga was incredibly hurt by what she saw as Max's careless attitude. Since then, she's been much more sensitive to Max's behaviour, looking out for evidence of his support – or lack of it. Focusing so keenly on Max's lack of emotional support means that the original pain grows as Helga increasingly experiences new hurts. Similarly, Vlad experienced James as uncaring during his father's illness and subsequent death, and feels James has never made up for that. Consequently, he finds it hard to forgive James and, like Helga, is sensitive to what he sees as further examples of uncaring behaviour. Neither Helga nor

Vlad can understand why their partners let them down, and they feel unable to forgive them. What happened is brought up regularly in arguments, though the more this happens, the less either James or Max want to talk about it. This inevitably compounds the insult, leaving Vlad and Helga unable to trust their partners or to feel they're dependable. What they're feeling is known as an 'attachment injury'.

Attachment injuries are not usually intentional, yet they're remarkably common. Few of us set out to make our partners' lives miserable or to create problems for ourselves, but it's really easy to trigger sensitivities we're not aware of. Acknowledging we've caused hurt often goes a long way to alleviating it. However, dismissing a partner's feelings because the hurt wasn't intended just makes it worse. Sometimes the incident which has been so traumatic might seem fairly trivial to an outsider, or might not even be remembered by the partner accused of it, but these events assume greater proportions because they feel like such a betrayal. They have such potency because someone trusted has proved unreliable. Not only has the expected helpful response not happened but the situation may have been made worse by denial that it caused hurt. Each time this happens it builds on previous attachment injuries in the person's life from which they haven't really recovered. This may go all the way back to early childhood when, somehow, the individual was let down by a parent or other close person. Each new hurt evokes all the others, perhaps making the latest incident feel like more than they can bear.

The incident that starts the trouble may have been a one-off behaviour or there may have been a series of let-downs that preceded this final straw. The only way this can be dealt with is to have a reparative experience which goes some way towards making up for what happened before. Of course, couple relationships already exist to a greater or lesser extent as reparative experiences for each of the partners, which is another reason why being let down is so devastating.

The partner who feels let down, and can't let go of the problem, is usually one who's very in touch with their feelings and likes to talk things through, while the other person may be someone who has also experienced attachment injuries in their life but deals with them very differently. They may be someone who's separated themselves from their pain and become very dismissive of what they see as vulnerability or neediness. Because they may actually have been *so* hurt in the past that they can't bear to connect fully with their feelings, similarly they can't bear to connect with someone else's pain, because it reminds them of their own. So they may manage poorly in a crisis or when their partner most needs them, often having no idea what they've done wrong and trivialising their partner's hurt response.

They'll be given an idea in no uncertain terms by some partners, but others just complain of feeling unsupported without mentioning the specific incident or what it was about the occasion which upset them. They may feel it's crucial that the partner realises by themselves the extent of the trauma they've inflicted or what it is about the event that was so shattering. Yet, even when partners do recall the incident, explain themselves and apologise, it may not be enough. The hurt partner often cannot be comforted and cannot forgive, and so the trauma continues for years and years and years.

It isn't difficult to see how couples can become locked into defensive patterns. Either may be afraid to risk showing any vulnerability or daring to rely on the other. Of course, the partner who tries to avoid anguish will be persistently exposed to it, causing their vulnerabilities to be triggered so that they need to use even more energy to manage their emotions, making them even less available to their partner. Remembering the incident may cause them to become upset and angry. Commonly, the trauma feels live and current. Indeed, it may feel as though there's danger all around. The loss of confidence that we'll be supported and cared for in our moments of direst need creates this feeling of ongoing trauma. The world feels less safe and certainty has vanished.

Discussing hurt

Because each partner comes to express their hurt feelings as anger and accusation, neither is ever able to express the authentic experience of hurt, vulnerability and loss which is the reason for all the pain in the first place. Being able to say what you each feel genuinely may seem too difficult, but organising your thoughts can break down something that feels overwhelming into more manageable chunks. Perhaps you could make notes on the aspects below:

- Why the incident was traumatic.

- The emotions you feel in connection with it. This will probably include current angry feelings, but see if you can remember how you felt at the time too.
- How this has changed your view of the world.
- What you needed at the time.
- What you need from your partner now.
- How all this can be managed going forward.

The partner who is thought to have been unsupportive could consider the following:

- Situations you find difficult or painful – anything which you feel you want to run away from or that makes you angry.
- If you weren't angry, what emotions you might be experiencing instead.

Loss

Losses which predated your current relationship can feel very live and can need just as much attention as incidents that affect both of you. Longing to be part of someone else's life and to share your experiences with someone who's on your side can almost feel like a physical pain after the loss of a partner. The years of experiences you shared are what made the relationship so comfortable and comforting. Feeling your way in a new relationship may feel so different that you can't imagine it ever working. Remember, however, that when your past relationship was new this uncertainty probably seemed exciting – there was so much to discover about each other.

It's also important to accept that you can't replace the partner you've lost, and you can't expect a new partner to fit into your life in the same way. It's difficult to compete with someone who died, so the loss of a partner can affect your current relationship enormously, especially if the new partner thinks you're comparing them – if you could, the first relationship wouldn't have been so special. As always, an open mind and curious approach will allow you to relax enough to enjoy what comes next instead of trying to recreate the past.

Losing a partner you had issues with may be even more difficult. It can be very hard to accept that they'll now never apologise, realise how much they hurt you or make amends. You'll never have the chance to tell them how you feel. Coming to terms with this can be incredibly difficult, and you may be irritable with your partner when unhappy memories or emotions are evoked. Then you can unfairly take out feelings about the previous partner on the new one.

You can't tell your previous partner how you felt, but you *can* take charge of your life going forward and make positive plans to have the life you want. The same goes for your relationship. You can negotiate how you want this to be and revisit this as often as you need to. Some sort of ritual ending may help too, such as writing down your feelings and burying them or planting a flower, tree or bush to tell your feelings to.

Other losses – parents, children, friends, pets – may also be affecting you and it doesn't help to ignore the grief you feel, as this just makes it more potent. Acknowledging how hurt you are and finding ways to express this can help. Marking anniversaries and other important dates can also be helpful, especially if you're able to share memories. This isn't always possible with a new partner but, though they can't share your memories, they may engage with your need to mark special days or gladly give you the space to do this.

Coming out

Coming out or even just questioning your sexuality or gender after one or more relationships isn't at all uncommon, though many people nevertheless worry about what their friends and family will make of it. If you've been in a straight relationship and have children, contemplating or finding yourself in a gay relationship will inevitably affect more than just yourself. Explaining what's happening to a long-term partner or your children isn't likely to be easy, though they may have guessed already. If this is out of the blue, though, it's much harder for you both. It may be that, having gone through a process of considering your sexuality and deciding to come out, or even just to experiment, you're feeling excited and relieved – but your partner and family may need time to adjust.

Your experience will affect the way they see themselves too, and they may express anger or grief as they try to work out what this means for themselves and for their relationship with you. It generally isn't a good idea to blurt the news out, especially to your children. If at all possible, it's always better to have a plan as to how the news will be broken, and to be interested in your children's response rather than demanding support. This allows them to feel they have some control over what's happening and reduces the gap in connection with you that's possible if the news is unexpected. Stick around after telling them so that there's time for questions and for them to realise that you're still the same person and that you love them.

If your partner comes out

Finding out that your partner is gay may make you wonder what the relationship was based on. Though a deep bond may remain between you, it's often hard not to be affected by what can seem like downright dishonesty. It can also feel very lonely if others are concerned about your partner and supportive of their coming out. You may then feel bitter that your feelings don't appear to be considered at all.

To say this is a shock goes nowhere near the complete sense of unreality some partners experience. Once the initial blow is accepted, the same feelings associated with straight affairs and feelings of betrayal have to be faced and you have to work out what and how much you want to share. This varies considerably. Oddly, it may be easier to come to terms with when you're in a long relationship where you're both confident that you have genuinely supported and loved each other, and probably still do. Sometimes – perhaps, ironically – it's the strength of a long relationship which has provided the confidence for someone to develop their feelings about the way they identify sexually.

When you haven't been together for long, on the other hand, it's easy to feel the whole relationship has been a sham. More people identify as pan-sexual or bisexual now, so it's more possible to become involved with someone who wants to be with you but isn't exclusively attracted to your gender. Having said this, it's less common now to be unaware of a potential partner's sexual identity, as it may be evident from social media. This needn't make a difference to the strength of your relationship and its potential to last, however. Organisations such as Straight Spouse Network (www. straightspouse.org) can offer support and information as you come to terms with what's happening.

Gender identity

Many couples in long relationships stay together after a partner begins to question their gender identity. Much depends on the strength of the relationship and the confidence of each partner to be honest about how they're experiencing what's happening. It doesn't necessarily follow that a trans partner will wish to have surgery, though they may want this or to make other physical changes which will involve new gender identification. They might not yet know how they want to proceed, so you could find yourself on this journey together. Depend (www.depend.org. uk) offers information and support for partners, regardless of the length of relationship. Trans relationships are discussed further in Chapter 12.

Any kind of relationship where you feel trust has been breached is bound to make you wary subsequently. In new relationships, personal disclosures may not be made until the relationship is becoming serious, which you may feel is rather late if you've already attached – so it's sensible to be open about what you want from the start. Though there'll always be some people who behave dishonestly, few deliberately set out to hurt. Being frank about what you expect from a relationship and situations you wish to avoid in future at least makes your own position clear. Indeed, it can't be emphasised enough that it's important to be explicit about what isn't acceptable to you, as new partners who seem similar to you may actually have a very different outlook.

Pornography

Pornography use can be a source of disagreement, for instance. Some people see it as equivalent to an affair while others take it for granted that their partner will occasionally use porn. Though it's by no means true that everyone enjoys porn, many people do, either individually or with their partner, so an opinion about its use has to be considered when embarking on a new relationship. If it's used for masturbation, it probably isn't going to come up in conversation very often, and abstinence is difficult to insist on if this doesn't affect you directly. You might, however, be concerned if you discover that a partner is spending several hours a week using porn or if you suspect it's interfering with your sex life.

It's very easy to become dependent on internet porn, and the risk of compulsion increases with use. It can affect men's ability to get and maintain an erection or to climax, as real partnered sex becomes less exciting than the larger-than-life images they become used to. Using internet porn for more than a few hours a week puts you at increased risk of developing dependency, causing changes to the brain with regular use (Birchard, 2015).

If you think your partner is affected, trying to make yourself more sexually available or attractive isn't usually helpful. Compulsive sexual behaviour isn't really about sex as such, but more about finding ways to ease stress, soothe distress or even just overcome boredom. The person will probably need professional help to kick their porn habit and to find other ways to manage their stress and low mood, together with the development of a more healthy lifestyle. You can find a therapist to help via the Association for the Treatment of Sexual Addiction and Compulsivity (www.atsac. co.uk), The College of Sexual and Relationship Therapists (www. cosrt.org.uk), Marylebone Centre for Psychological Therapies (www.marylebonecentre.co.uk), Relate (www.relate.org.uk) and Sex Addicts Anonymous in the UK (http://saauk.info/en). They should all be able to help partners as well.

Many people with so-called addictive personalities have had some sort of trauma in their lives, which needs to be addressed if treatment is to be successful. Often, they have other compulsive habits, such as shopping or gambling, behaviours such as alcohol or substance abuse, or enjoy risky activities or sports. Any of these may have financial implications as well as implications for the time you have available to spend together. The habits may have existed for many years, and are certainly likely to predate a short relationship. The main problem for you as a partner may not be the behaviour itself as much as the deceit that can often accompany it.

Love addiction

This may be even more the case if your new partner is affected by love addiction. This may have a sexual component, but is usually characterised by loss of interest when the excitement associated with the early part of a relationship begins to wear off. As we've already learned (pages 14 and 68), this 'honeymoon period' is when bonding hormones cause huge excitement and feelings that a relationship is special. The partner's shortcomings are overlooked and it may be difficult to think about anything but the relationship.

As the hormones start to wear off and reality kicks in, some people feel the need for a return of the early relationship excitement or, alternatively, believe that their change in feelings signals that the relationship is not 'the real thing'. Indeed, some people seek counselling to discover why they lose the feelings after a certain period of time. The truth is that this highly intense period is unsustainable. As with sex addiction, some sort of past trauma may be what's really preventing a love addict from becoming close to someone else. All of this may make you more wary about embarking on a new relationship, especially if you feel out of touch with sexual matters, something which is discussed in the next chapter.

Remember: Any sort of trauma from the past can emerge and disrupt a relationship many years later. The older we are, and the more relationships we've had, the more likely we are to be carrying emotional baggage that may need to be addressed.

Bibliography

Birchard, T. (2015) *CBT for Compulsive Sexual Behaviour*, Hove: Routledge.

Hilton, D. (2013) Pornography addiction – a supranormal stimulus considered in the context of neuroplasticity. *Socioaffective neuroscience and Psychology* 3. www.socioaffectiveneuroscipsychol.net/index.php/snp/article/view/20767. Accessed 19 November 2015.

Chapter 11

Sex

Having a sexual relationship again after a break can be daunting. Though some people begin again with no qualms, making the most of their freedom, others feel more uncertain. You may not have expected to have to negotiate dating and sexual etiquette ever again, and in a new long-term relationship there's a lot to discover. The longer it's been since your last new relationship, the more apprehensive you may feel.

You may feel less confident about your body, especially if you've gained or lost weight or had body-altering surgery. However, your new partner may be having similar thoughts about themselves, so do be honest about any doubts and reservations at an early stage. Few of us have the perfect beach body, and neither will the partners you meet. It's really hard to define what each of us finds attractive. While the perfect body may be a turn-on, personal preferences are very quirky and most people are ultimately most turned on by the relationship. To boost your confidence and make you feel sexier, it helps to focus on a body part that you like and to make the most of it.

There may be medical reasons to maintain a healthy body weight but, beyond that, 'acceptable bodies' are socially created. Fashionable body shapes and sizes have changed throughout history and are different in different countries and cultures too. There's no actual arbiter of what is culturally acceptable, but we buy into the notion that there is. Some of the sexiest people, who glory in their sensuality, don't have conventionally beautiful body shapes, at least by contemporary Western standards. Moreover, the idea of naked bodies touching is erotic regardless of the way the bodies look, especially if those bodies belong to people who care about each other and choose to express this physically. Remember that, if your partner is enthusiastic and appreciative of your body, it's you who is creating a problem if you let yourself feel ashamed of it. Nonetheless, if you aren't ready for sex, don't rush it. You'll both have a better experience if you've become more relaxed and trusting.

Sexual boundaries

Unfortunately, conversations about sexual boundaries seem to happen less when couples are reluctant to admit they're more than acquaintances. Given that relationships are so public now, where relationship status is often announced in your online profile, there isn't the space to just wait and see where relationships are going privately. It's often easier to call the relationship casual than to have a tricky discussion that might be disappointing or seem pushy. Consequently, relationships these days are often sexual long before couples agree they're an item. This allows sexual problems to develop unaddressed and makes it difficult to bring them up later. It's especially difficult if you haven't been sharing your sexual preferences and needs, but don't want to hurt your partner's feelings by starting to ask for changes.

Many couples' sexual repertoire becomes increasingly limited because they rule out anything that isn't always accepted enthusiastically. Indeed, sex therapist David Schnarch (2009) says many couples' sex lives just consist of the 'leftovers' that remain once couples have set up no-go areas. However, tastes and moods change and there's no harm in suggesting something different. An honest conversation, rather than continuing to make assumptions, may allow more sexual experimentation or the occasional resumption of some off-limits practices. If you find talking uncomfortable, sexual role-playing will sometimes allow you to say and do things you'd find difficult as yourself. You might have a lot of fun just coming up with a role play scenario too.

Anal sex

If you'd been in a relationship for many years, you may fear that new partners will expect more of you sexually or that you won't know what to do. There's been a great deal in the media about increased pornography use changing sexual behaviour. However, it's more likely that people who've used a lot of porn, especially at an early age, will have difficulty with loving partnered sex than that they'll be especially skilled or expect you to have exotic sexual tastes. Anal sex is often mentioned as a modern variant, and some men and women do love it. Others do not. Research about its prevalence varies wildly, so don't be coerced into thinking this is something 'everyone' does. There's a theory that some people want to try it or offer it because it's something they've never done before, so in a second relationship it could be seen as equivalent to loss of virginity. However, you absolutely shouldn't engage in any sexual activity that doesn't appeal to you, and it's abusive for a partner to coerce you to do something you don't want to.

If this is something you've always wanted to try, however, you must use a condom. There are extra-thick ones, especially for anal sex. The anus is fragile and full of bacteria so it's essential for both partners to use protection. Use tons of lube, and start gently, stimulating the anal area with just a finger or tongue (use dental dams). Rest the penis for a while once inside, so that the body has time to relax and accommodate the penis. Experiment with comfortable positions and don't thrust too hard and fast, as this can cause tearing. Stop if either of you experiences more than a little discomfort. You need to change the condom – and ideally wash penis and hands – if you follow up with vaginal sex.

With anal sex or other new practices, including kink, don't wait to discuss what you want until you're actually in bed. Planning is vital, especially including agreement about when to stop. This is especially important with role play or kink where part of the 'story' you've agreed may include sexual coyness. Consequently, you need to agree safe behaviour and words to end or pause. Do research and use proper equipment, rather than improvising, if you're interested in bondage or sadomasochism, to ensure confidence and safety.

Sexual frequency

Another issue for new relationships may be a mismatch in expectations about sexual behaviour and frequency. If you and your former partner were satisfied with sex every few months, but your new partner wants to make love several times a week, you'll need to find a compromise. Sexual frequency is often seen as a relationship barometer, so it can certainly cause disappointment and unhappiness as well as pleasure and joy. However, this is often due to the pressure individuals and couples place upon themselves to have not just frequent enough sex but spectacular sex. It doesn't take much insecurity or performance anxiety to start worrying and either pestering for more sex, putting pressure on your partner to show they're enjoying themselves more obviously or to avoid sex altogether.

Avoiding sex is often a result of performance or response pressure – worrying about being a good enough lover, climaxing too soon, not at all or taking too long. It can be surprisingly helpful to agree not to have sex for a short time but to concentrate on building intimacy, enjoying cuddles and maybe even some delicious kisses. Couples often avoid physical touch in case it's construed as a prelude to sex, so a sex ban can allow intimacy to grow unfettered. You might progress to having a bath together or sleeping naked and introducing sexual touch gradually, agreeing not to focus on orgasm or intercourse, at least initially. This way your confidence is given a chance to grow and you can take time to learn about one another's bodies and responses. By the time you lift the sex ban, you're likely to be much closer, more trusting and more physically comfortable with each other.

Trust and physical comfort is important, because a really enjoyable and successful sexual relationship requires each partner to take responsibility for their own pleasure. This means being prepared to tell and show your partner what you enjoy rather than just hoping they'll get it right. If you've had very few sexual partners, you may be surprised at how different sex is with another person, which you may find exciting or terrifying. Rather than worrying about what you don't know, try to see discovering the uniqueness of each other's bodies as an erotic adventure, not a test or trial. Do talk about your doubts and take things slowly to allow your trust and confidence to build. Or just go for it and do what comes naturally, if that seems right for you. There's no correct or perfect way to go about lovemaking. Many people feel that the most mind-blowing sex they have comes from a loving connection rather than an impeccable technique.

Sexual problems

You may expect a recurrence of any sexual issues you had during your last relationship, such as difficulty with orgasms or erectile problems. However, they often disappear or diminish, as a poor relationship can seriously affect sexual functioning. Even the newest partners are usually more than willing to help overcome sexual barriers. In fact, discussing your concerns, and working together to create a sexual relationship you both enjoy, will help to improve your overall communication and problem-solving skills. It may even promote better sexual functioning than would have been the case without some issues.

It's essential to discuss condom use, whatever your age, and dental dams if you're having oral sex, to reduce the risk of infection, particularly if either of you have been sexually active since becoming single. You need to ask about sexual infections, as some people don't automatically disclose them if they're practising safer sex. Conversations about the exclusivity of the relationship are important too. It shouldn't be assumed that your new partner wants a monogamous relationship, nor that they don't.

Female orgasm

Considerable pressure is often experienced if you worry about 'getting it right', both in new relationships and in longer ones where you might feel sex has become a little stale. If you've never had an orgasm, you may now feel you should. However, if you're happy as you are, don't be pressured – but do be prepared to talk about this in case your partner fears you're dissatisfied. If you decide you do want to orgasm, experimenting with a vibrator together or by yourself can be a great start.

Many couples also still believe they should climax simultaneously or that women should be able to orgasm during intercourse. The reality is that, though some women do orgasm during intercourse, very few climax without some form of additional clitoral stimulation. The part of the clitoris that's visible is only the tip. It's a much more complex organ, internally extending on either side of the vulva and providing a complex area of nerves which may be felt as a small bump along the upper wall of the vagina, known as the G spot. When very aroused, these areas become blood-engorged and sensitive. Hence, so-called 'vaginal orgasm' actually becomes more likely when a woman has already climaxed. While direct clitoral stimulation may be uncomfortable immediately following orgasm, stimulation of the vulva and G spot may be pleasant and quickly cause orgasm. The area around the urethra is also highly sensitive, and stimulation here can lead to 'ejaculation' from glands near the urethra. The G spot can also be stimulated digitally, using two fingers in a 'come hither' motion.

Women's preferences and sexual needs are all different, and the same woman may want to be stimulated differently not just on different occasions but from moment to moment. It's therefore unlikely that partners will always correctly work out what's needed, nor is it reasonable to have fixed expectations about women's sexual responses. Open-mindedness, experimentation and willingness to talk about preferences and needs help tremendously.

Male orgasm

Men have orgasm problems too. Some have difficulty ejaculating in front of a partner or during intercourse. There are many factors contributing to this, which commonly include:

- early sexual experience of a partner's distaste;
- sexual abuse;
- shock when they first ejaculated and weren't expecting this;
- being teased or in trouble over wet dreams or masturbation;
- fear of pregnancy;
- too much porn use;
- or an idiosyncratic masturbation style which partners can't replicate. For instance, boys who share a bedroom or fear discovery often develop a quick, efficient masturbatory technique which sometimes becomes the only way they can climax.

Sometimes, men also appear aroused because of their erection but are actually very anxious, something that's more likely in a new relationship. Nervousness can affect how soon they climax, though many couples have unrealistic expectations of how long a man should be able to continue thrusting. The average is only a couple of minutes, and few men go on for more than five. If you both like a lot of intercourse, withdrawing just short of climax and continuing partner stimulation before resuming intercourse is the way to keep going. It isn't considered 'early ejaculation' unless you climax virtually as soon as you penetrate or even earlier. This often happens due to nervousness or because a man is unable to recognise his 'point of inevitability', the moment beyond which ejaculation can't be prevented. Ability to recognise this sometimes diminishes as men age too. Slow stimulation, noticing the sensations being experienced, helps men to notice when they're about to climax. Eventually, you'll learn to stop, wait a while and then resume, which can result in a more intense orgasm, as well as improved ejaculatory control.

However, it helps considerably if you don't see penetrative sex as 'real sex' or as an essential part of lovemaking. It can be a wonderful part, but it doesn't have to happen every time. Nor, indeed, does orgasm. Stressing about it can, in itself, cause sexual problems and distract you from the pleasure and intimacy of the overall experience.

Erections

Problems with erections are highly associated with performance anxiety. One lost erection can lead to a lifetime of worry about whether the erection will be reliable next time. This anxiety can be all it takes to prevent the erection or lead to early ejaculation. Some men are so focused on being able to keep an erection long enough to climax that they rush sex and a quick climax becomes a habit. Equally, worrying about erection isn't sexy and can affect arousal, making climax unlikely.

Often, men have erections on waking in the morning and no problem masturbating, but anxiety leads to less reliable erections with their partner. However, loss of morning erections and consistently unreliable erections can be an early sign of cardiovascular disease, so it's always a good idea to have this checked out with your GP. GPs can also run simple blood tests to check hormone levels.

Many men seek drugs like Viagra to give them reassurance. Though they can be very helpful, they sometimes aren't really necessary. As men age, their erections become less firm and tend to come and go more during a sexual encounter. Though it may be completely normal, this can be seen as a problem when neither partner expects it. It's easy enough for the partner or man himself to give a little more stimulation to regain the erection if it's required. However, some couples feel inhibited about the man touching himself, or the partner may not realise that more stimulation is needed, so you must talk about this if it bothers you. An erection isn't necessarily a sign of how aroused the man is, and partners shouldn't see erection loss as a sign that they aren't desirable.

Schedule sex

Many couples have completely unrealistic expectations of sex and their bodies, and need to take a far more relaxed approach. Spontaneity is also highly valued, though this actually stalls sex for many people. Issues of hygiene, mood, time and place can make sex seem unattractive or awkward at a particular moment, so the partner is pushed away in case seduction progresses. Then the couple may end up not even having a cuddle.

Rather than mistime your advances and be disappointed, it makes more sense to schedule sex or some sort of intimate together time. You can make this special, whether or not it includes sex, with soft lighting, candles, incense, body oils – be creative. Some couples take a little picnic up to bed or into the bath, with tasty treats like olives, strawberries, chocolates and sparkling wine. Creating a special occasion when there's enough time to enjoy it makes partners feel special too.

Separate rooms

If you've been single for a long time, the idea of sharing a bed with someone else may be really off-putting. You may snore, have hot flushes or restless legs, need the loo a lot during the night or suffer from insomnia. You may just not be used to sharing anymore. Though you may quickly get used to sharing again, preferring separate rooms shouldn't be a reason to avoid relationships or sex. Some couples with separate rooms have a cuddle every night in bed before they go their separate ways, or they make intimacy more of an occasion by inviting one another to visit their room.

The attitude you both adopt is what makes separate rooms work. If you think positively about what you're doing, it won't be a problem. You're both more likely to get a good night's sleep plus lovely cuddles and sex when you want it. It's how we think we *should* feel, and what we think we *ought* to be doing, that creates the majority of problems with sex. There isn't actually anyone with a rulebook, so you need to do what feels right and possible for your unique relationship.

Desire

Companionship may be higher on your agenda than desire, of course. Desire tends to be discussed as something that's intrinsically just there. It's therefore often assumed that there's something wrong if we don't have it. However, desire results from circumstances that go way beyond biological sex drive. For some people, feeling really close is important, but closeness can create performance anxiety instead of desire. Some people like a slow burn, building up to lovemaking over a flirty few hours or even days. Other couples only make love after a row, while yet more only feel relaxed enough for sex when they're on holidays.

All sorts of factors inhibit sex – children or parents in the house, pets around, a full stomach, too much to drink. Some inhibitory factors only develop or reveal themselves as the relationship progresses. Becoming used to each other's preferences is part of getting to know each other and may need adjusting to. It doesn't mean you're sexually incompatible, just that your differences may need to be taken into account.

Women's desire tends to fade in longer relationships, regardless of their age (Basson, 2000). This doesn't reflect their love, the attractiveness of the partner or their arousal once they start making love. Desire follows arousal for some men too, so couples in long relationships may have to make more effort to timetable sex or cuddles. Of course, wanting to make love also depends on it being a pleasant experience, but for some people sex involves pain.

Pain

There are many reasons why sex may be associated with pain. Sometimes, fear of pain makes people reluctant to attempt sex, and it's impossible to relax and just enjoy it when they do. In women, painful intercourse can make them so tense that penetration becomes impossible. Some also develop vulval pain, either all the time or when touched, especially round the entrance to the vagina. Some women have never been able to use tampons or have intercourse, often due to an initial painful attempt or particularly tough hymen. Sometimes, pain develops post-childbirth, perhaps due to having had stitches or just fear. For other women, painful intercourse is due to conditions like endometriosis, where cells like those which line the womb are found elsewhere, or scarring from previous infections or surgery. Some women have mid-month pain when they ovulate, and urinary or pelvic infections can cause pain.

In post-menopausal women, vaginal dryness can be such a problem that extra lubrication is needed. If you haven't had intercourse for a long time, there may be post-menopausal changes in the vagina which make penetration difficult, requiring considerable patience. Don't just put up with this. See your general practitioner (GP) to find out whether a gynaecological referral would help you. Sex therapy may also be of benefit.

Men experience pain too. A tight foreskin can make sex extremely painful, and infection can make the penis very sore. It's important to be scrupulous about hygiene, including rolling back the foreskin to wash underneath and drying the penis after weeing. Some men experience chronic pelvic pain, for which a cause can rarely be found, but which can make sex very uncomfortable.

Men facing prostate surgery often worry about their sexual functioning afterwards. For some, it takes a while to feel their bodies are in any way behaving themselves, especially as their ejaculate goes backwards into their bladder post-surgery, causing cloudy urine. Not apparently ejaculating with orgasm can be quite disconcerting to both partners, but this is completely to be expected. Nonetheless, it's always worth seeking a medical opinion if you're worried after any clinical procedure, if only to put your mind at rest.

Many people just put up with their concerns and pain. However, there's much that can be done to help, both in terms of medical treatment and psychological support. It's most important to try to get a diagnosis, so do see your GP or specialist as soon as possible to get the ball rolling. In common with all the sexual problems described here, sexual pain often leads to psychological issues, including avoidance and fear, which may persist long after the cause of the pain has been treated. Psychosexual therapy can be very helpful; therapists can be found via Relate (www.relate.org.uk) and the College of Sexual and Relationship Therapists (www.cosrt. org.uk).

Whatever they are, sexual concerns shouldn't be a reason to give up being sexual. Sex produces endorphins which improve well-being and numerous other health benefits, such as a reduced risk of prostate cancer and dementia. What's more, many people consider they have their most relaxed, anxiety-free sex later in life, and older people often have more frequent and satisfying sex. Frequency is not something to worry about, though couples often become concerned if sex becomes more or less frequent. But relationships do change over time, and the next chapter explores the idea that relationships have a lifecycle.

Remember: Sexual success is about being able to relax and enjoy whatever works for you and your partner, rather than putting yourselves under pressure to perform.

Bibliography

Basson, R. (2000) The female sexual response: A different model. *Journal of Sex and Marital Therapy*, 26, 51–65.

Schnarch, D. (2009) *Intimacy and Desire*, New York: Beaufort Books.

Chapter 12

Love and the relationship lifecycle

Once an important relationship has ended, most of us are concerned not to repeat the mistakes of the past. However, it's easy to confuse normal changes in the relationship lifecycle with problems or to write off developing issues as inevitable and unimportant. For instance, many couples complain that something changes once the initial excitement of the early relationship has passed. Indeed, some people are so convinced that they should be able to sustain the heightened feelings of the so-called honeymoon period that they actually end relationships when the intensity fades.

Limerance

It isn't possible for relationships to sustain their early 'limerance', a state that produces a very pleasant kind of obsessive infatuation and continues for up to a couple of years. During this time, the body produces endorphins which cause that delightful heady feeling that the world is a better place with the two of you together in it. The hormones prevent you from seeing each other's flaws and you allow yourself to believe your partner may provide the fulfilment of all your hopes and dreams. Enjoy this stage; it's about to end. The purpose of all the loving endorphins flooding your body is to make the two of you bond and have sex. With luck, you'll reproduce.

This disappointingly unromantic explanation does fit events. For instance, the honeymoon period often begins to wear off as soon as you start seeing more of each other, become pregnant, move in together or make some other form of commitment. From nature's point of view, your bond is then established and normal service is resumed. This is why, if you have doubts about your relationship in the early days, progressing it is unlikely to allay your fears. Instead, the post-honeymoon period is when many couples realise that their partner isn't the answer to all their prayers and that their early promise won't be (entirely) realised. This can lead to a process of grieving, which is exacerbated these days by the spotlight of social media. The effort of appearing to have the perfect relationship may actually cause relationship problems.

Commitment

Typically, in the post-honeymoon stage, couples become resentful and argue about minor issues, avoiding addressing their deeper feelings of disappointment. It's at this time too that many couples start a family, commit to an expensive home or accept demanding work, thereby adding to the stress they experience, but also providing distractions. For newly joined older couples, this phase may coincide with life changes such as retirement, having grandchildren, reduction in income, losing or nursing a parent or managing their own poor health.

It's difficult to avoid external pressures which stress relationships, and easy to blame the relationship for succumbing to pressure. Rather than finding ways to address this, many couples struggle on hoping that, once they're through the current phase, the relationship will somehow work itself out. Though some do stay blissfully loved-up, this may have much to do with their own ability to address negative thoughts and feelings and work realistically on their issues, learning from their experience. Couples like this are usually secure in their own skin and don't rely on each other to make them feel good, though they enjoy being in a relationship and are able to give and take appropriately. For everyone else, relationships may be considerably harder than expected, and new partners may turn out to have more shortcomings than we'd ever imagined possible.

Negotiating

It's usual to experience peaks and troughs in your relationship, including times when you don't know why you bother. Few relationships survive for long without encountering crises; how these are resolved may be the key to relationship health and longevity. The more able couples are to approach problems collaboratively, the less likely they are to blame and criticise and to enjoy each other's company. This allows the later years of relationships to be calmer, as couples become more trusting of each other and their ability to weather stresses.

Indeed, couples in long, largely happy, relationships are notably respectful of each other and take responsibility for their own part in relationship distress. They may be more inclined to think about solutions and how *they* could change, rather than waiting for the relationship to evolve or for their partner to be different. The quiz below offers a quick illustration of whether you're inclined to take action or hope for the best.

Quiz: Are you a hoper or a healer?

1. You've been dating for six months and your new partner suggests you move in together. Do you:
    a)   Start packing.
    b)   Suggest more long weekends staying together to see how that goes.
    c)   Start worrying about whether you're ready, but feel unable to say no.
    d)   Say you think the relationship's fine as it is.
2. As your new relationship progresses, you're starting to find your partner a bit boring. Do you:
    a)   Argue about their lack of energy and enthusiasm.
    b)   Try to plan some more interesting activities together.
    c)   Feel you've made a mistake but have to put up with it.
    d)   Carry on with your own life and enjoy your friends and family.
3. You don't get on with your new partner's adult daughter. Do you:
    a)   Complain about her to your partner.
    b)   Try to get to know her better and see if you can get on.
    c)   Feel hurt that your partner doesn't realise how much she upsets you.
    d)   Try to have nothing to do with her.
4. Your partner seems a bit distant. Do you:
    a)   Tell them they're being rude and inconsiderate.
    b)   Mention that something appears to be wrong and say you're available to talk if they want to.
    c)   Worry that you've done something to upset them.
    d)   Book couple counselling.

5. A relative of yours is unwell and you want to visit them. Do you:
   a) Insist your partner accompanies you.
   b) Discuss what's happened with your partner and decide together whether they come with you.
   c) Feel you can't go as it would mean leaving your partner alone.
   d) Just go.
6. You snore very loudly and your partner suggests separate bedrooms. Do you:
   a) Refuse – what's the point of a relationship if you sleep apart?
   b) Agree, but ensure you still have bedtime cuddles.
   c) Agree, but feel very hurt.
   d) See if your general practitioner (GP) can recommend a cure for snoring.

Mostly As

You know your own mind and actively pursue your dreams. However, you could slow down a little and make sure your partner hasn't been left behind. You may see their genuine needs and wishes as failure to appreciate *your* needs and wishes. Try to assume less and make more decisions jointly to avoid resentment on both sides.

Mostly Bs

You do your best to consider other people's feelings and point of view. You need to be clear about your boundaries and ensure you're not the only one managing emotions in the relationship, however. Do make sure you can ask for what you need too.

Mostly Cs

You don't like to be a bother, so you fall in with your partner's wishes rather than being clear about your own needs too. You may feel hurt by your partner's failure to recognise how hard you're trying, but they may not realise that you don't agree with them. Being more assertive would benefit you both in the long run.

Mostly Ds

You don't let the grass grow, believing that problems are there to be fixed. You know your own mind and make your position clear. However, sometimes it might be worth checking that your partner is on board with your solutions. You might enjoy sharing the responsibility occasionally rather than feeling you have to provide all the answers.

Boredom

It's not unusual for the middle part of relationships to be characterised by boredom. Ironically, the more important you become to one another, the more boring the relationship may become. Couples often settle into a routine and fear that seeking change may suggest they aren't happy. There may also be little time or energy for change, and few couples are good at making space to review their relationship. So they carry on, not rocking the boat, until something happens which provides a legitimate reason to change – such as the children leaving home, retirement or ill-health. Then, and only then, will some couples dare to suggest their lives together could be different. This may mean developing more shared interests and activities, allowing one another to sometimes pursue separate paths, fulfil bucket lists or return to study. It may mean moving house, to a different part of the country or even abroad. It may even mean recommitting to exactly the life you already have. After this renegotiation, many couples feel life is better than ever, and wish they'd taken it in hand much earlier.

For some couples, there isn't just boredom but actual unhappiness that goes unaddressed, and which could easily lead to (potentially avoidable) dissatisfaction and resentment. For instance, familiarity often leads to loss of intimacy, feeling unappreciated, or uncertainty about someone's value to their partner. It often doesn't take much to provide reassurance, yet it can be really difficult to know how to start a conversation about this. If so, do seek couple counselling as soon as cracks appear rather than waiting for the relationship to get worse.

Many partners assume counselling isn't an option before their relationship is on its last legs, but relationship therapists advise that early intervention can nip problems in the bud. Talking to a third person may be easier than just talking to your partner, and a qualified relationship therapist will help you find ways to start conversations in future and think differently about what's possible. For instance, for relationships to be successful, both partners need to be able to ditch their assumptions and develop genuine curiosity and interest about each other's thoughts and behaviours in order to accommodate differences. Otherwise, they can be together for decades feeling disappointed and hurt, when a little exploration and compromise would have helped. However, it's never too late to change and even long, difficult relationships can be successfully turned around.

Living together apart

Sometimes, a conventional relationship trajectory isn't appropriate, especially for second-timers. For some couples, for instance, the idea of commitment creates its own problems. Some people feel uncomfortable being too close while others don't want to lose their freedom, especially if their individuality felt stifled in a previous relationship. It's tempting to give in to pressure from your partner, friends and family to formalise your relationship, when it's actually fine as it is. It makes sense to live together if you're growing a family but may be less important if you already have one and are balancing your commitments to elderly parents and adult children as well as to your new partner.

Your relationship may not need to accommodate other family members in the way that relationships do if either or both of you have dependent children or parents who help with childcare. If you do have dependants, you'll have decided when it's appropriate to introduce your partner, probably only wanting to involve them with your children if you're sure they're going to stick around. But if they aren't managing a blended family and they can afford to, many couples now compromise and live together part-time or spend periods away pursuing their own interests or visiting their families. Whether you choose to be together full-time or not, it pays to be sure about what you want and to discuss it honestly.

People who feel burned by their last relationship or who have grown used to their own space may particularly favour living apart. This may be considerably better than letting the relationship just settle into the doldrums, with neither of you happy but not having the energy or inclination to leave or to make changes. Such relationships can rub along quite nicely if you both have personal activities to occupy you and sufficient shared pastimes and beliefs to avoid being at loggerheads. Unfortunately, the interest that many couples share is arguing, and they repeat the same row until the day they die.

Some couples are exposed to more criticism than others, placing even greater strain on their relationship (Blount and Young, 2015). Examples would include same-sex couples, those with an age gap, different religion or ethnicity, disability or other health issues, and differences in social class and education. Recognising external pressure or discrimination means there's less chance of blaming each other for any resulting distress. Some couples even find their relationship is strengthened, while others find it impossible to manage. To some extent, even if there is some disapproval, other family and community support may influence how well you cope. Even if you're managing, it's important to monitor the effect on you both. Prejudice and bigotry are never acceptable, but sometimes someone who has, unfortunately, grown used to this may not appreciate the effect it can have on a new partner.

Polyamory

Apparently similar couples actually often have a mismatch of experience. If you don't begin exploring your gay sexuality until later in life, you may still be applying heteronormative expectations that aren't necessarily appropriate, for instance. Gay men, in particular, are more likely to need conversations about how they manage other sexual relationships, if they have them, which many do without damaging their primary love relationship. About half of gay men and bisexual individuals and up to about a third of straight couples openly have more than one partner (Barker, 2013), and there is some evidence that polyamory may be more acceptable among older people. This may be a matter of convenience – a case of friends sticking together because it suits them, feeling there is no longer any point in worrying about conventions. Sometimes relationships are emotional rather than sexual, sometimes both, and sometimes the primary relationship is emotional and others are sexual.

It's hard to know, because it's so rarely talked about, but there may be many more polyamorous relationships than we're generally aware of. In many ways, polyamory makes sense, especially if you're older and have grown families. Many people with more than one relationship say they feel less jealous and clearer about the relationship boundaries than they do in dyadic relationships. They also feel more secure. The more close friends you have, the more likely it is that you'll always have a plus one to accompany you when you need one, companionship and a shoulder to cry on when one becomes necessary. There may also be more support available should you become ill or need help for some reason.

The point really is not to feel that you have to do your next relationship in a stereotypical way that you imagine is 'right'. Going forward, you can explore what seems 'right' for you and your partner(s) and do your best to make that work, because there isn't a magic formula that will ensure everything is perfect next time.

Trying again

Sometimes your next partner turns out to be your previous partner. Time apart can help to hone understanding of your needs and make you both more tolerant. If a couple have both developed during their break, they may have a much better understanding of each other and find their previous shared history gives them a head start as a couple. Being clear about how you want the relationship to be is important, and it won't work if you can't give up resentment about how it was before, how it ended or what happened while you were apart.

Many people whose partner's trans identity emerges during their relationship want to continue to be together as they don't feel their gender identity affects the strength of their relationship. Continuing the relationship isn't as straightforward as this may sound, of course, as both partners will experience a kind of adolescence as they each discover a new individuality and relationship, and there are no guarantees that it will work. Nonetheless, many couples find that it does, provided they can be honest about their expectations and aware that these may change. Gender Trust (https://helplines. org/helplines/the-gender-trust) is a great first stop for information and advice.

Case study: Laura and Lynn

Laura met Eric through a mutual friend who thought they'd get on as they'd both recently ended long relationships. They did get on well and saw a great deal of each other during the next couple of months, both feeling the relationship was a full-blown love affair. They were on their first holiday, three months after they'd met, when Eric told Laura that his marriage had ended because he'd told his wife he identified as trans. Both she and Eric's children had been unable to accept this, though they all later became supportive.

Though Laura was initially heart-broken by Eric's news, she found herself delighted that Eric wanted their relationship to continue. They made the final decision together for Eric to begin treatment to transition. Though she loved Eric, Laura realised the person she was *in* love with was Lynn. Laura, nonetheless, found it difficult to imagine herself in a lesbian relationship and worried about the reaction of her family. However, the strength of her relationship with Lynn, and their happiness together, convinced her that labels were irrelevant. It didn't matter what the relationship was called, it was the relationship itself that counted.

Arranged marriages

Arranged relationships account for more than half the marriages globally (Starbuck and Lundy, 2015) and follow the same sort of lifecycle trajectory as so-called love marriages. Part of the reason they're so successful may be because couples expect to have to work at their relationship and because they have the support of their families and community. When they don't work, however, the individual partners can sometimes feel cut adrift from this support and feel that they offer a less attractive relationship prospect going forward.

The reason for the relationship ending may influence whether you want to remarry at all, let alone how you meet your next partner. There's no reason why another relationship shouldn't work, but you should be careful not to put too much pressure on yourself. Both individual and couple counselling to explore what you could do differently next time may be very helpful. Some people find it useful to experience both religious and secular counselling in order to compare their approaches and determine what works for them.

Going forward, you may feel it's necessary to balance your own needs against and with the needs of those around you. For instance, it may be very important to consider your family's wishes if they're nearby, but they may not understand your life so well if they're in another country. If you decide to find your own partner, you may be encouraged not to let the voices of concerned new friends entirely displace those of concerned family. Ultimately, what you choose to do is up to you, but there may be times when you'll appreciate an advocate if your wishes clash with the expectations of others.

A new family

This isn't very different to the kinds of choices many people feel they have to make when they enter a new relationship if they have existing family commitments that need to be accommodated. For instance, if you've already raised a family you may not be so keen to start another, and worry about the reaction of your existing children, while your partner may be desperate for a family of their own. Don't coerce each other into making decisions that could ultimately damage the relationship if they aren't what one of you wants. For instance, it's understandable, if you want children, to feel that time is running out if you or your partner is a woman in her late thirties or forties. However, you ultimately need to think about whether the relationship is convenient because you want children or that you want kids because this is a forever relationship.

If having children has long been a priority, it's easy to lose sight of what trying to have them means. There may be fertility problems, a higher risk of foetal abnormality, as well as difficulty funding and enjoying two families at potentially different stages. It can also be tough to find the energy for all this when your contemporaries are winding down and taking life more easily as their families start growing up. What's more, all this is likely to be happening during the second to sixth years of your relationship, which are when you should be dealing with your disappointment that the relationship isn't perfect and working out how to be together. Having said this, not trying if this is something you badly want will leave you always wondering about what might have been. Just keep checking that what you thought you wanted still works for you.

Spillover pressure

Even first relationships have probably never been subject to so much stress. Ironically, pressure to be fulfilled and have it all can make life even harder as partners berate themselves for finding this so difficult. Roles are much less clear and partners' expectations may be very different.

There's now no doubt that stress has a detrimental effect on health and that relationships often bear the brunt of this. Sudden flare-ups obviously cause acute pressure, but many relationships experience chronic stress, so there's no chance to recover from any crises. What's more, spillover stress is caused by not having enough time to spend with partner or children but feeling that home and family life interfere with work. The pressure individuals place on themselves to perfectly fulfil their roles as both partners and employees is exacerbated by the additional pressure partners actually create when they believe the other is not managing home/work conflict appropriately. For instance, one may resent that the other is not home from work earlier, leaving them missing companionship, dealing with household chores or childcare and missing out on family life. The cause of resentment is usually that each partner's self-image is damaged when they fail to achieve the impossibly high standards they set themselves, usually blaming their partner's lack of support for this, rather than the situation in which they both find themselves.

Most of us are barely, if at all, aware that we have such high standards or that we push ourselves and each other so hard. Yet this is a major cause of relationship conflict, particularly in second and subsequent relationships where pressure to get it right may be overwhelming. Partners in relationships where roles are clear are not nearly as affected by this sort of stress, so it makes sense to work out what's realistic and possible and to discuss respective responsibilities rather than making assumptions. Stress, jealousy and competition over each other's children and ex-partners provide yet more strain during early relationships, and the needs of children or elderly relatives can seem to take over at times.

Though many couples do have wonderful relationships despite these circumstances, they're usually realistic people who are already able to communicate well and who are good at problem-solving together. They anticipate problems and have ideas about how these could be managed long before they occur. They won't expect each other's children to like them, though they'll be pleased if they do, and will keep remembering that *they* are the adults. If you're ready for this, and don't feel knocked off course if your new partner has preoccupations with people other than you at times, the relationship will probably do very well.

Planning for loss

To futureproof your new relationship even more, you could consider how you'll manage if one of you becomes ill, especially if there's a big age difference and/or no children. It's worth thinking about what sort of support you might both need, whether you'd be prepared to move, where to and how your current roles may need to be modified. Being brutally honest, decide before you commit whether your relationship could survive a major illness or upheaval. Also remember that you may be alone again one day and that it's important to maintain other relationships, however loved-up you are. It's crucial to know one another's wishes regarding end-of-life issues and funerals to avoid clashes with other family members when the time comes.

All this may seem morbid when you're embarking on a new life together, but thinking ahead gets the conversation over with early on and means you have clear plans to help you when it's necessary. A lovely idea is to tell the other person your hopes about how their life would be if you were to die first. For instance, you might hope your partner would talk to your photo occasionally, wear red on Tuesdays in your memory or try to visit your grave or special place on your birthday. It's important not to create rigid rules that would be difficult to follow, but simple requests can be incredibly comforting and can help keep your relationship alive, as will happy memories. How to create happy memories and make the most of your new relationship is the subject of Chapter 13.

Remember: Relationships are dynamic and have a changing lifecycle. Staying curious and interested, and taking responsibility for your part in your relationship's welfare, will help to maintain its health.

Bibliography

Barker, M. (2013) *Rewriting the Rules*, London: Routledge.

Blount, A. J. and Young, M. E. (2015) Counselling multiple-heritage couples. *Journal of Multicultural Counseling and Development*, 60, 137–152.

Starbuck, G. H. and Lundy, K. S. (2015) *Families in Context: Sociological Perspectives*, third edition, New York: Routledge.

Chapter 13

Happy Ever After

Once you've found your next partner, a new issue may arise – what will it mean if this relationship ends too? Though the concept of living happily ever after comes from fairy tales, the belief that a romantic relationship will make life better is reinforced everywhere, with 'normal' life portrayed as sexually coupled. In comparison, other relationships can appear inferior, so some people still regard singletons as unfortunate and the divorced as morally polluted. Moreover, many of us feel like failures, and inevitably socially damaged, if we aren't partnered.

Cynics might argue that the concept of romantic love is a great way to persuade people to put themselves through many years of hardship, exhaustion and tedium while they raise their families and prioritise each other. After all, widespread serial relationships and demands for higher pay and recognition of the demands of homemaking and childcare would place much greater demands on the community/state. As it is, we tend to blame our partners when the washing up isn't done, when we're bored, exhausted or feel unappreciated. What we don't do is blame the daft idea that one person can meet *all* our needs *all* the time.

Relationships are good for us though. Physical and mental health benefits from companionship, entertainment, sex and from knowing that we're special to someone. Appropriately, research in 2017 revealed that married heart patients, particularly men, have lower mortality rates than single patients. Some of this is because couples encourage treatment compliance, reminding one another to take medication, exercise, eat healthily and report symptoms. They may also feel they have more to lose. Nonetheless, successful relationships require effort.

Most of us were unprepared first time round for the difficulty of living with someone else in what is inevitably an extraordinarily demanding relationship. As the previous chapters have demonstrated, it's often our expectations of perfection that help to make it all so hard, and this sets us up for dissatisfaction and resentment. It can be harder still if there's unfinished business from a previous relationship, such as a sudden ending. The more you learn about how to make relationships work, the more regret there may be that you never got the chance to try in the past. Those who've been widowed often feel disloyal in new relationships and either expect to be judged or find themselves making comparisons. It's really important, however, to realise that no two relationships are the same. A long relationship that began in your youth is very different from one that starts when you've acquired life experience separately. In youth, couples discover the adult world together; in later life, they discover each other.

It's very easy to assume you know how relationships work and to embark on new relationships with expectations carried over from the old ones. You'll each have a 'normal' way of living, probably with different habits, attitudes and tastes. Just because some may coincide, it doesn't mean they all will. Being open to difference rather than set in your ways may mean co-creating a new normal. This can involve making major decisions – about where to live, for instance – or maybe just about accommodating small habits and preferences.

Laila and Jim

Jim looked forward to reading the weekend newspaper on his own for an hour or so after breakfast. The first time he settled down to do this, his new partner Laila told him he was lazy. An argument followed, during which Laila made it clear that she didn't expect Jim to 'put his feet up' while she cleared away breakfast. Jim genuinely saw this as a deal-breaker, as he really felt the space and peace this gave him was essential.

Laila, meanwhile, felt this was selfish, as she'd been hoping they'd go for a walk. As a compromise, she suggested they clear breakfast together before looking at the papers. Perhaps they could go for a walk the next day? Maybe they could stop at a café and read the papers with a cappuccino? Though he was aware it seemed unreasonable, Jim's initial response was to refuse to alter his routine, which he felt he *needed*. Laila felt Jim was rude, and was treating her 'like a maid'. Jim had all week to read the paper, she argued, and the weekend should be couple time. They agreed their relationship wouldn't work.

When Jim settled down to read the paper the following Saturday morning, something had changed. He didn't feel comfortable and couldn't concentrate. He wondered if he'd made a mistake. After a while, he called Laila and asked if she wanted to go for a walk. It turned out they both wished they'd handled things differently. In the end, they agreed the best way to avoid arguments like this in future was to develop a plan about how they'd spend their time together rather than each having their own expectations.

Having a plan

Talking through what you expect to happen, whether it's a date or how to spend your time after work, avoids the kind of arguments experienced by Jim and Laila. Indeed, planning can help avoid conflict in most situations, as it involves considering what might go wrong as well as clarifying expectations and knowing what to do and when to do it. It's surprising how many people resist the idea of planning on the basis that they value spontaneity or just like to see how they feel. However, the reality of this frequently means doing nothing. In the case of difficult situations, such as family occasions which often end in rows, just hoping that it'll be different this time isn't going to help. Providing activities which offer distractions or avoid people drinking too much might do the trick though.

Planning needn't mean avoiding spontaneity. A good plan means alternatives will have been taken into account; for instance, what will you do if it rains during a picnic? You can plan for mood too; if you feel tired you'll have a barbecue at home, but if you feel energetic you'll go for a walk and a pub lunch, for instance.

It's a good idea to consult everyone involved in an event. You may be thrilled with your plans, but just check they work for everyone, as it's impossible to think of all the requirements they may have – access to water to take medication, frequent loo stops, somewhere for babies to nap at specific times, for example. Knowing what you're dealing with is much better than surprises that derail all your plans. If you start doing whatever it is and have a better idea, or need to change something, do it. Starting out with a plan *allows* spontaneity rather than stifles it.

Bigger plans for how you want to live your life can also be help-ful, particularly if you're deciding whether to live or spend more time together or if you feel your relationship is becoming stale. It's important to identify which aspects of your life mean the most to you or enhance your wellbeing and how your partner fits into this. The exercise below may help.

Exercise: What kind of life do I want?

- What does your typical day involve? How could/does your partner fit into this?
- When your partner's around, how do they make your day bet-ter? How do they get in the way?
- What would you like to do differently? How would your part-ner facilitate this?
- How do I see my future? How does this differ from my partner's plans?
- How do I like to spend weekends and holidays?
- How much time do I need to spend alone?
- What activities are essential to my wellbeing? What would I like to give up?
- How do family and friends fit into my life? How does my part-ner affect this?
- How does my partner affect my pets?
- How are my values and beliefs reflected in the time spent with my partner?

You may feel that your dissatisfaction is the fault of your relation-ship or that your relationship could solve your dissatisfaction. In fact, this exercise often shows that there's much you could do to make changes by yourself or that some effort is needed to ensure you're able to accommodate one another's needs appropriately – or even just to recognise what your needs are. Another helpful exercise considers the way you affect each other. Completing the sentences below can help you to work out what your differences are and whether anything needs to be done to accommodate them.

Exercise: I am the kind of person

- I am the kind of person who... and my partner changes this because...

You might, for instance, say: *I am the kind of person who enjoys shopping and my partner changes this because she gets impatient when I browse.* In this case, maybe shopping together isn't such a good idea, as neither of you seems to enjoy the experience. Or maybe your partner could have a coffee while you shop, or you could meet at the end of a shopping trip for a meal or other activity. Many couples share activities because they feel they ought to, perhaps thinking it's the sign of a strong relationship. However, if it isn't a good experience, it doesn't serve the relationship well.

- I am the kind of person who... and my partner supports this because...

Someone else might write: *I am the kind of person who enjoys shopping and my partner supports this because she gives me a lift to and from the shops.* This doesn't say what the partner does while the person is shopping, whether they mind giving lifts or whether, in fact, the lifts prevent the person from shopping with a friend. In other words, this very simple statement potentially has many layers of complexity that could be usefully explored.

- My partner is the kind of person who... and I am different because...

Another statement could be: *My partner is the kind of person who likes to be quiet and I am different because I find silence very difficult, and always have the radio on.* This statement suggests there's a dilemma because there's difference. We don't know, though, whether solitude with the radio is what this person needs, whether they would like to talk with their partner more or whether the partner makes them turn off the radio.

The three statements can refer to feelings, behaviours or attitudes and it's most useful to write some relating to all three. It's helpful to be curious about them rather than just accepting what they say, and to wonder what else they could mean and what questions they might raise. Sharing with your partner can be useful too, as it can help you to work out what isn't being said and what you still don't know. You might consider whether you'd like to be able to write a slightly different statement, and what would have to happen to make the difference.

It can also be interesting to just think about what isn't being said. This might be something you want to know, something that always causes a row or something upsetting. It's worth thinking through what might be different if you did talk. Some couples collude into old age to avoid discussing something they believe may take them outside their comfort zone or even threaten the relationship, such as an affair, loss of a baby, a legal offence, problems with a relative or their sex life. Not talking may seem like a solution, but it leaves you both never knowing if you could have made something better, settled feelings or resolved a hurt. Rowing about the subject may seem to address it, but many couples just repeat the same script over and over, which airs the pain but does nothing to resolve it.

Mindful relationships

It's too easy to carry a negative focus into your next relationship, often the result of fear that it may not last. Instead, make it a habit to scan your life and relationship, noticing what does work rather than what doesn't. Notice what you enjoy. Notice the roles you both play in the relationship. For instance, you may get a buzz from your job, your gliding hobby and catching up with friends, but worry that there's something wrong with the relationship because your partner isn't involved in any of these. However, if you're coming home to snuggle up with your partner and feel at peace, and if neither of you is dissatisfied with the arrangement, what's the problem? If your partner feels neglected, on the other hand, you may have some renegotiating to do, with yourself as well as your partner. Would you rather give up the peaceful life your partner provides or would it be helpful to have a few more nights out (or in) with your partner instead of friends?

The more comfortable you feel together, the less you may feel the need to nurture the relationship. However, it may slip away under your nose unless you spend time investing in it. Some people feel very awkward commenting on their partner or relationship, but appreciation is priceless. Try to notice and thank each other if you help one another or show consideration. Simply remarking that you're having a good time when you're together offers reassurance and acknowledgement that you're sharing. Be gracious when you're offered compliments and appreciation, and be sure to reciprocate when it's appropriate.

Make sure, too, that you make time for intimacy. Whether this just means cuddling up on the sofa or lots of mind-blowing sex, try to touch often. Just ensuring you have little rituals for bedtime, greetings and farewells helps to top up wellbeing and benefits overall health. Make time to talk and try not to avoid subjects that worry you. Don't go on and on in your need for reassurance, but do mention anything you want to change or that's hurt you, rather than hoping for the best. Some of the suggestions in earlier chapters make it simpler to have a routine that facilitates good communication.

Remember: Don't worry. Even if your new relationship doesn't last forever, you can have some fun, learn more about yourself and perhaps you will have made a lifelong friend.

Bibliography

Carter, P., Uppal, H., Chandran, S. and Potlun, R. (2017) Married patients with modifiable cardiovascular risk factors have lower mortality rates. *Heart*: Supplement in *British Medical Journal*, 103, A68.

Index